ALWAYS GAVE FORGIVENESS

The Legacy of Peggy Mew Who Always Forged
Her Own Path as written by her daughter

DEBBIE DOBBINS

NEVER ASKED PERMISSION

For information contact:

Debbie Dobbins

https://thedebbiedobbins.com

Book and Cover design by Designer

ISBN: 979-8-9923327-1-1

First Edition: January, 2025

ACKNOWLEDGMENTS

A life spanning nine decades creates a tapestry woven with countless threads of friendship, love, and shared purpose. While my memory may not be as sharp as it once was, my heart remembers clearly the people who have touched my life in profound ways.

First and foremost, to Sandy Gray, my dearest friend and spiritual travel companion - our adventures from Greece to Israel have enriched my life beyond measure. Your friendship has been one of God's greatest gifts to me.

To Peter and Jackie Amundson, whose generosity in opening their home for countless Republican fundraising events went far beyond political support. You became family in all but name, and your friendship remains one of my life's treasures.

Celeste Greig, you have proven that true friendship can weather any storm. Our bond has only grown stronger through the challenges we've faced together, and I am grateful for your unwavering presence in my life.

My spiritual family at Calvary Chino Hills - Judi Neal, Gina Gleason, and Pastor Jack - you continue to provide guidance and inspiration even as miles separate us. Your teachings and friendship reach across the distance to touch my heart in Texas.

To Cindy and Ray Wilson, my Monrovia neighbors from the beginning - decades of Fourth of July celebrations and shared memories have created a friendship that feels eternal. You've been there through all of life's seasons, and I treasure every moment.

The Mountjoy family - Gary, Judy, and Dennis - your love for Dick matched my own, and your dedication to continuing his legacy touches my heart deeply. Our shared memories and ongoing connection mean the world to me.

Christopher Lancaster and family, watching you grow from a child on Nearglen to the person you are today has been one of life's special joys. Your continued friendship bridges generations and reminds me of the lasting impact we can have on each other's lives.

Linda Boyd, what began as an accidental connection through your husband blossomed into one of my most cherished friendships. You've proven that life's best gifts often come in unexpected packages.

Steve Johnson, your constant presence in my life, from California and beyond, exemplifies the rare quality of enduring friendship. You've been a true friend among friends.

To Pam Duffy, our friendship transcended your connection to Warren and grew into something beautiful and lasting. You've shown me how relationships can evolve and deepen over time.

My heart is full of gratitude for so many others who have shared this journey - Earl and Judy Devries, Holly Carver, Jane Warner, Jeff and Cathy Evans, Linda Daggett, Nancy & Tony LeNeis, Joanne McIntosh, Rhonda Ryder Brown, Tom Cross, Tim Donnelly - and countless others who have made my journey through politics and life one of joy, purpose, and lasting friendship.

Though these words can only capture a fraction of the gratitude I feel, please know that each of you holds a special place in my heart. You've helped shape not just my story, but the very essence of who I am.

With deepest appreciation and love,
Peggy.

TABLE OF CONTENTS

INTRODUCTION

This biography began as conversations between a mother and daughter, recorded over several months in 2024. As I, her daughter Debbie, sat with my mother Peggy Mew, listening to her recount nine decades of life, I discovered layers to her story that even I, having lived through much of it, had never fully understood. What emerged was not just a chronicle of one woman's life, but a testament to the resilience and adaptability that defined a generation of American women who refused to be limited by society's expectations.

Born in 1937 in Denver, Colorado, my mother's story unfolds against the backdrop of transformative decades in American history. From her early years as a spirited child finding creative ways to skip school, to becoming a young military wife managing four children on a strict budget, to her emergence as a formidable force in California politics, her journey reflects both personal determination and the changing role of women in American society.

The intimacy of our conversations allowed me to capture not just the events of her life, but the spirit and energy that drove them. Through her voice, we experience the pride of the "paper lady" supporting her family through ingenuity and hard work, the dedication of the political organizer who helped shape California conservative politics, and the joy of the "button lady" who found new purpose in Texas. Her story carries us from the streets of post-war Denver to the halls of California's State Assembly, from family camping adventures to international travels, and finally to her role as matriarch in Wichita Falls, Texas, where she continues to influence and inspire four generations of her family.

This is not a tale of unbroken triumph - it's honest about the struggles, the setbacks, and the hard choices that shaped her path. Through our conversations, my mother shared both her successes and her vulnerabilities, painting a portrait of a life lived with fierce independence, unwavering determination, and deep love for family and country. Her story, told through a daughter's lens but in her own voice, offers insights into how one woman's journey reflected and influenced the American experience across nine decades of profound change.

As you read these pages, you'll hear the voice of a woman who never waited for permission to make her mark on the world. From the young girl who learned to sew without a machine to the grandmother who organized political campaigns from her lift chair, my mother's story reminds us that every life contains multitudes, and that our greatest legacy lies in the lives we touch and the examples we set for generations to follow.

Chapter 1

THE BEGINNING
EARLY YEARS IN DENVER

The year was 1937, and the world was a different place. Franklin D. Roosevelt was in the White House, the Golden Gate Bridge had just opened, and in a modest house in Denver, Colorado, I, Peggy Ragsdale, took my first breath. It's funny how the circumstances of our birth, the time and place we enter this world, shape so much of who we become. I may not remember that day, but it was the start of a journey that would take me places I never could have imagined.

Denver in the late 1930s and early 1940s was a city on the cusp of change. The Great Depression was slowly releasing its grip, and there was a sense of cautious optimism in the air. But for a young girl like me, the complexities of the adult world were far removed from my daily life. My world was much smaller, centered around family, home, and the adventures I could find in our neighborhood.

My earliest memories revolve around our house on the outskirts of Denver. It wasn't much by today's standards, but to me, it was home. We had a small yard where I spent countless hours playing, and the streets of our neighborhood became the backdrop for countless adventures.

My brother Jack was my constant companion in those early years. Three years older than me - though sometimes just two, depending on the time of year - he was a natural leader with a mischievous streak that would often lead us both into trouble. I was his willing accomplice, eager to keep up with my big brother and prove that I was just as brave and daring as he was. Looking back, I realize now that many of our "adventures" were probably giving our parents gray hairs, but at the time, it all seemed perfectly reasonable.

Our parents both worked - my father as a bus driver and my mother as a waitress at a restaurant-bar down the street. Having both parents work wasn't as common then as it is now, but that was our reality. They would leave for work each day, and we were supposed to go to school. That "supposed to" became a rather flexible concept, thanks to Jack's innovative thinking.

One of our most memorable escapades involved our creative interpretation of school attendance. Jack discovered a storefront on the main highway where other kids would gather. I was under ten at the time, and instead of heading to school, we'd make our way there. The place became our unofficial clubhouse - just a bunch of kids with too much time on their hands and not enough supervision. We'd spend our days playing, somehow managing to get lunch, and then carefully timing our return home to coincide with when school would normally let out.

Our parents would come home from their long days at work, thinking we'd been diligently attending our classes. The deception worked perfectly - until it didn't. One day, the truth arrived in the mail, exposing our truancy to our parents. The consequences were far more serious than we had imagined. Our parents were summoned to court, where the judge delivered a stark ultimatum: either they ensured we attended school, or we would be taken away from them.

The solution came in the form of Catholic school. The court's logic was simple - if our parents had to pay for our education, they'd make certain we attended. This meant a new daily routine: taking the streetcar down Main Street, then another up Colfax Avenue to reach the school. No more playing hooky in storefronts; our days of freedom had come to an end.

Catholic school was an entirely different world. Jack, having already received his first communion, was granted privileges I didn't have. He could participate in church services and join in the singing, while I had to stand in the back of the room. I learned all the songs but wasn't allowed to sing them - a small but memorable frustration that stuck with me.

Life in wartime Denver added another layer to our childhood experiences. The shadow of World War II loomed large, even in the mind of a young child. I remember the hushed conversations of adults, the worried looks exchanged when the radio news came on. Although the fighting was far away, its effects reached even our small corner of Denver.

Rationing became a part of daily life. I didn't fully understand it at the time, but I knew that certain things were harder to come by. Everyone had to adapt, and even children became aware of the sacrifices being made for the war effort. Despite the restrictions, Jack and I still found ways to entertain ourselves - some more legitimate than others.

The movie theater became one of our favorite destinations. The shows would change every Saturday and Sunday, giving us two opportunities each weekend for entertainment - if we could get in. The admission was only nine cents, but even that small amount was often beyond our means. Jack, ever resourceful, would figure out ways for us to sneak in. Looking back, I realize I was quite the willing accomplice in these schemes. He had a way of getting me to go along with his plans, and I never seemed to put up much resistance.

Our neighborhood was our playground, and despite the challenges of the times, there was a sense of community that seems rare today. We knew every street, every shortcut, every potential adventure spot. The winters were particularly memorable - Denver would transform under a blanket of snow, and to a child's eyes, it was like waking up in a different world. The cold never seemed to bother us much; we were too busy exploring and creating our own entertainment.

But beneath the surface of our childhood adventures, changes were brewing. The dynamics of our family were shifting in ways I didn't fully comprehend at the time. My parents' marriage was struggling, though as children, we were largely sheltered from the details. It wasn't until I was approaching my tenth birthday that the full impact of these changes would become clear.

The decision that would alter the course of my life came when my parents chose to separate. My brother Jack decided to stay in Denver with our father, while I would accompany my mother to California. It was a profound split - not just of our family, but of my childhood world. Jack would stay to finish school in Denver; he wanted to attend the college there and had dreams of working on a ranch, which he eventually did. He was a good young man, and though our paths would diverge, the adventures and mischief we shared in those early years would always bind us together.

The journey from Denver to California was my first real adventure on my own - just my mother and me on a bus, lasting three days. I remember it took what felt like forever, and the buses back then weren't anything like they are today. They didn't even have bathrooms; we had to stop frequently throughout the night for bathroom breaks. We were carrying everything we could bring of our life, probably all fitting into a single suitcase. It was both exciting and terrifying, heading toward a completely unknown future.

Bus from Denver to California

Looking back on those early years in Denver, I'm struck by how different the world was then. It was a simpler time in many ways, but also a time of great change and possibility. The foundations of who I would become were being laid, brick by brick, experience by experience. Each adventure with Jack, each scheme we concocted, each challenge we faced - they all contributed to shaping my character.

I learned resilience from watching our parents work hard every day to provide for us. Even when we were skipping school (something I certainly wouldn't recommend), we were learning independence and resourcefulness - traits that would serve me well throughout my life. The Catholic school experience, while not entirely welcome at the time, taught me about structure and discipline, even if I had to learn it the hard way.

Those early experiences in Denver gave me a strong foundation, a sense of who I was and where I came from. They instilled in me values and beliefs that would guide me throughout my life. And most importantly, they sparked a curiosity about the world, a desire to learn and grow, that has never left me. Even our rebellious streaks - the truancy, the sneaking into movies - reflected a spirit of adventure that would later express itself in more constructive ways.

The war years, though difficult, taught us all about adaptation and sacrifice. Even as children, we learned to make do with less, to find joy in simple pleasures, to create our own entertainment. These lessons would prove valuable throughout my life, teaching me that happiness doesn't depend on having everything you want, but on making the most of what you have.

Living in Denver during that time also taught me about change - how quickly it can come, how dramatically it can alter your life, and how important it is to be ready to adapt. When the time came to leave for California, I was only ten years old, but I had already learned some crucial life lessons about resilience and adaptation.

The decision to separate our family - with Jack staying in Denver and me heading to California with my mother - was perhaps the most significant change of my young life. It was a split that would shape both our futures in profound ways. Jack would go on to attend college in Denver and fulfill his dream of working on a ranch, while my path would lead me to entirely different adventures on the West Coast.

As I prepared to leave Denver, I couldn't have imagined the life that awaited me in California. I couldn't have known that the curious, adventurous little girl from Denver would grow up to travel the world, to become involved in politics, to raise a family of her own. But that's the beauty of life - each chapter builds on the one before, each experience shaping us, molding us, preparing us for what's to come.

The memories of those early years in Denver have stayed with me throughout my life - the adventures with Jack, the streetcar rides to Catholic school, the snowy winters, and even the challenges we faced as a family. Denver will always be a part of me, the place where my story began. And though my journey would take me far from those familiar streets, the lessons I learned there, the experiences I had, would remain with me always.

As that bus pulled away from Denver, carrying my mother and me toward California, I was leaving behind more than just a city. I was leaving behind my childhood, my brother, and a way of life I had always known. But I was also carrying with me the strength, resilience, and sense of adventure that life had installed in my DNA. These qualities would serve me well in the years to come, helping me adapt to new situations and face whatever challenges lay ahead.

Life has a way of taking unexpected turns, of leading us down paths we never anticipated. That ten-year-old girl on the bus couldn't have known what the future held, but she was ready to face it with the same spirit of adventure that had characterized her early years in Denver. The journey that began in 1937 was just beginning to unfold, and California would open up a whole new chapter in my life.

Chapter 2

COMING OF AGE IN CALIFORNIA

The journey west in 1947 marked more than just a physical move from Denver to California - it was a journey from childhood to something else entirely, though I didn't know it then. That three-day bus ride felt like an eternity to a ten-year-old girl. The buses in those days weren't equipped with bathrooms or air conditioning; they were simply long metal tubes rumbling down highways that seemed to stretch forever. We had to stop throughout the night for bathroom breaks, and every stop reminded me that we were getting farther from everything familiar - my brother Jack, our neighborhood, the life I had known.

California in the late 1940s was a state transformed by the war years. The defense industry had brought waves of newcomers, and cities were expanding rapidly to accommodate them. My mother and I were just two more faces in this migration, carrying what little we could of our old life in a single suitcase. She had already secured a job at Nash's Department Store, and her boyfriend, whom she'd met while working as a waitress back in Denver, was waiting to pick us up when we arrived.

Our first home in California was a room at the Alhambra Hotel, just around the corner from Nash's. It seemed promising at first - a fresh start in a new place. But California had early lessons to teach me about self-reliance and awareness. One day, while my mother was at work, there was a knock at our hotel room door. When I asked who it was, a man's voice answered, "Just let me in." Then came the chilling words: "I have a key." The fear I felt in that moment taught me something about trust and caution that would stay with me forever. I waited, ready to run, but thankfully, he couldn't get in. When I told my mother about the incident, we quickly moved to another motel on Valley Boulevard.

That first year became a series of moves, each one prompted by the approaching due date of rent. From the motel where the owner killed chickens for our dinner to an apartment above a store, we were constantly in motion. It might sound unstable to modern ears, but at ten years old, I saw it all as an adventure. Every new place brought new discoveries, new neighbors, new ways of living. Looking back now, I realize how hard my mother must have worked to maintain an air of adventure rather than letting the uncertainty overwhelm us.

School in California presented its own kind of culture shock. The Catholic school education I'd received in Denver, despite my attempts to avoid it, had actually put me ahead academically. In these post-war years, California schools were bursting with baby boom children, struggling to keep up with the rapid population growth. Walking into Garfield School, I found myself in larger classes than I'd known in Denver, but with the surprising advantage of being able to help other students with their work.

EASTER BUNNY ASSISTANTS — The Las So nadoras club is among the many service clubs at AHS which are planning Easter vacation activities for hospitals and orphanages. Mary Helen Pearne, second from left, Club presiden t. and Peggy Ragsdale. member, give the Easter bunny an assist by helping. from left. Mary, Adele and Diane, color Easter eggs

Peggy Helps Kids as a Teenager

This academic success, however, would soon be interrupted by something no one could have predicted. The first bout of rheumatic fever hit like a thunderbolt in an otherwise clear sky. The late 1940s were still an era when such illnesses could be devastating - before the widespread use of antibiotics, before the medical advances we take for granted today. When my mother took me to the doctor, his immediate response was to send me to Los Angeles General Hospital.

The doctor called for an ambulance, but even sick as I was, my pride wouldn't allow it. The thought of neighbors seeing an ambulance, of becoming the subject of local gossip, was unbearable. "No," I insisted, "I don't want to ride in an ambulance." In those days, children weren't given many choices about medical care, but somehow my protest worked. We took a taxi instead, my small victory against the public display of illness.

Los Angeles General Hospital in the late 1940s was a world unto itself - a sprawling complex that served everyone from the wealthy to the indigent. My roommate turned out to be a girl from Juvenile Hall, which we could actually see from our hospital windows. She was nice enough, but when I innocently told my mother about my "really nice" roommate from Juvie, my hospital stay came to an abrupt end. Mother got the doctors to release me, deciding home care was preferable to such influences.

Recovery meant strict bed rest, a challenge for any child but particularly for one used to constant motion. Our home then was upstairs in a house on an Alhambra street, and the neighbors who owned the downstairs portion became unwitting surveillance agents. Every time a car drove past, I couldn't resist getting up to look out the window. The neighbors would report these unauthorized expeditions to my mother, but their monitoring only made me more determined to catch glimpses of the world going by.

The second bout of rheumatic fever came during my teenage years, just when I was discovering tennis and a taste for independence. The early 1950s were a time of renewed energy and optimism in America, and I was determined to be part of it all. Perhaps I pushed too hard, didn't rest enough - teenagers rarely think about such things. This time, the illness left me with a heart murmur that doctors warned would be permanent. Their dire predictions included the declaration that I would never be able to have children, a statement that would prove remarkably wrong in the years to come.

Life in 1950s Alhambra had its own rhythm, distinctly different from today's fast-paced world. The streets were lined with modest homes, many still sporting victory gardens from the war years. Television was just beginning to appear in living rooms, but teenagers still made their own entertainment. I found my first real California friend living across the street from our upstairs apartment, and together we discovered the art of teenage rebellion, 1950s style.

Our adventures weren't always well thought out. One particular incident stands vivid in my memory - my friend became convinced her father was hiding something in some mail, and she was determined to open it. With all the wisdom of my teenage years, I advised her that if she was going to open it, she'd have to throw it away afterward. She had what seemed like a better idea - steaming it open. Armed with a match for heat and more curiosity than sense, we attempted our amateur sleuthing, only to accidentally set the curtains on fire. The arrival of the fire truck certainly added excitement to the afternoon, though explaining it to her father was considerably less entertaining.

But it was our walks down Main Street that truly defined our teenage rebellion. In an era when young ladies were expected to be demure and proper, we would don shorts and bright fluorescent shirts - mine lime green, hers shocking pink - and parade up and down the street, counting the whistles from passing cars. We never walked alone; that was our one rule. We didn't want to actually get picked up - we just wanted to be noticed. Looking back now, it seems almost innocent compared to modern teenage exploits, but in the conservative 1950s, it was quite the statement.

Jobs came early in those days. The movie theater on Atlantic Boulevard became my first regular employment, earning twenty-five cents an hour. This was the golden age of cinema, when movies were still a major social event. The theater itself was a magnificent single-screen palace, nothing like today's multiplexes. The air was always heavy with the smell of popcorn and possibility, and even working there felt like being part of something magical. These were the days of James Dean and Marilyn Monroe, when every movie premiere felt like a cultural event.

Peggy 14 in Alhambra

But it was during one of those walks down Main Street, in my lime green shirt, that fate would take a hand. Jerry and Jim Dobbins happened to be driving by that day. I was just another teenager trying to get noticed, but somehow this particular notice would change everything. The Dobbins family would become more than just employers or acquaintances - they would become the family I hadn't known I was looking for.

It was Jerry's mother Betty, (who would later become my kids "Grammy") who first saw something in me that perhaps I didn't yet see in myself. Betty arranged for me to work as a live-in babysitter for a family in San Marino, a position that would open my eyes to a world vastly different from the one I'd known. San Marino in the 1950s was the epitome of post-war prosperity - a world of manicured lawns, gleaming American-made cars in circular driveways, and homes that looked like they'd stepped out of Better Homes and Gardens magazine.

Betty (Grammy) had a way of taking people under her wing, of seeing potential where others might not look. Perhaps she recognized in me something of herself - a determination to make something of life regardless of circumstances. She became more than just my soon to be mother-in-law; she became a guide to a world I was just beginning to understand.

Grammy and Bapa with Peggy

The contrast between my previous life of constant movement and the structured elegance of San Marino was stark. Here were families who'd lived in the same house for generations, children who'd never known the uncertainty of next month's rent. While I missed my mother, living in this environment taught me valuable lessons about different social classes and how they operated. I watched, I learned, and I began to understand that there were many different ways to live in this world.

The 1950s were an era of rigid social structures, but they were also a time of possibility. Working in San Marino, I straddled two worlds - the help who lived in, but also a young woman observing and absorbing everything around me. I learned the unspoken rules of upper-class society, the proper way to serve tea, how to navigate social situations I'd never encountered in my previous life. These skills would prove invaluable in my later years, though I couldn't have known it then.

The late 1950s were a time of profound social change in America. The rigid structures of the immediate post-war years were beginning to crack, though the real social upheavals of the 1960s were still to come. I was caught in this transition, a young woman shaped by hardship but increasingly exposed to opportunity. The girl who had once moved from motel to motel was learning to navigate cocktail parties and formal dinners, all while maintaining the core of who she was.

The transformation from the girl who arrived on that bus from Denver to the young woman catching Jerry Dobbins' eye was more than just a coming of age - it was a complete metamorphosis. By the late 1950s, I had developed a confidence that came not from privilege but from necessity. My stint in San Marino had taught me how the other half lived, while my own experiences had taught me how to survive. This combination would prove invaluable, though I didn't know it yet.

The walks down Main Street in those fluorescent shirts seem almost prophetic now - a bright signal flare announcing a readiness for change. While other girls my age were planning their senior proms or thinking about college, I was already living in a more adult world. The skills I'd learned - from managing on my own while my mother worked, to navigating the refined world of San Marino, to understanding how to move between social classes with ease - had prepared me for something, though I wasn't sure what.

Betty's presence in my life grew stronger, her guidance more purposeful. Looking back, I wonder if she saw in me a potential she recognized, or if she was simply following her instincts about her son's future. Either way, her influence would prove pivotal. The woman who would become Grammy to my kids was orchestrating a future none of us could have predicted.

The late 1950s hung suspended between the rigid conformity of the post-war years and the social upheavals to come. Elvis was starting to shake things up on the radio, and teenagers were beginning to question the strict social rules of their parents' generation. But I was about to skip right over the typical teenage rebellions and straight into a different kind of revolution - one that would transform me from a girl in a fluorescent shirt to a mother before I'd even had time to finish being young.

That day on Main Street, when Jerry and Jim Dobbins drove by, was more than just another afternoon of seeking attention. It was the pivot point between my childhood and what would come next. At seventeen, I thought I was grown up - had been pretending to be grown up for years, really. But real adulthood was about to arrive with a speed and intensity that would take my breath away.

Chapter 3

YOUNG LOVE AND STARTING A FAMILY

The summer air was still warm that evening when Jerry first asked me out, and the scent of night-blooming jasmine hung heavy in the air. I was seventeen, thought I knew everything, and had no idea that my whole world was about to change. The girl in the lime green shirt was about to discover that growing up wasn't just about looking grown up - it was about facing life's challenges head-on, ready or not.

Marriage at seventeen wasn't uncommon in 1954 - it was the era of young brides and starter homes, of rushed weddings and hopeful beginnings. Our wedding date - December 7th, Pearl Harbor Day - seemed to foreshadow the military life that lay ahead. The holiday season of 1954 was a whirlwind of new beginnings: a new bride in a suit rather than a white dress, Christmas decorations twinkling in windows, and unknown to me at the time, a new life already beginning.

That first Christmas as Mrs. Dobbins had barely passed when I discovered I was pregnant. While other young women my age were making New Year's resolutions about finding romance or starting careers, I was facing 1955 with the knowledge that I would become a mother before the year was out. Those doctors who had so confidently declared I would never have children due to my heart murmur were about to be proven spectacularly wrong.

The timing of that first pregnancy seems almost poetic now - a Christmas bride carrying new life through the spring and summer, my own personal miracle despite medical predictions. Jerry was in the Navy, and military life waited for no one. Soon after our wedding, we headed to Washington state where he had to join a minesweeper boat. The young bride who had never left California except for that long-ago bus ride from Denver was suddenly navigating military bases and Navy protocol, learning a whole new language of ranks and regulations while simultaneously learning about pregnancy and impending motherhood.

The early months of 1955 were a crash course in growing up quickly. While the rest of the country was watching "I Love Lucy" and worrying about the Space Race with the Soviets, I was facing my own personal revolution - managing morning sickness on a military base, preparing for a baby while my new husband prepared for deployment, and learning that being a military wife often meant being on your own.

Pregnancy in 1955 was a different world from today's experience. There were no ultrasounds, no prenatal vitamins, no *What to Expect When You're Expecting*. Just monthly doctor visits where they'd listen to your heart - in my case, with extra attention due to that troublesome heart murmur - and tell you to eat well and rest. But rest wasn't easy to come by when your husband was shipping out and you were learning to navigate military life on your own.

Being pregnant in those first months of 1955 while living on a military base was an education in itself. The base had its own ecosystem of young wives, many of us expecting our first children, all of us learning to navigate this new life together. My mother's experience as a waitress had taught me about independence, and Grammy's influence had shown me how to adapt to different social circles, but nothing had quite prepared me for the unique culture of military life.

Valentine's Day came and went with Jerry at sea. By Easter, I was showing enough that my spring clothes needed letting out. Through it all, the other Navy wives became my lifeline. We'd gather for coffee in each other's small base housing units, sharing pregnancy symptoms and war letters, comparing notes on which doctors were best at the Corona Naval Hospital. Some of these women were barely older than I was, but military life had a way of aging you quickly - not in years, but in experience.

The Spring of 1955 felt like summer, sweltering in Southern California, and my pregnancy progressed through those hot months with all the typical discomforts magnified by military housing that wasn't always well-cooled. But there was a certain pride in handling it all, in proving those doctors wrong with every kick and movement I felt. Grammy and Bapa (what we called the kids grand father Donald who my son Don was named after) became increasingly excited about their first grandchild, and their support was unwavering.

By late summer, when Jerry's minesweeper was somewhere in the Pacific, the reality of giving birth without him present became a real possibility. Military wives learned to face these possibilities with stoic determination - it wasn't what you wanted, but it was what might need to be done. The Corona Naval Hospital became my second home with frequent check-ups, the doctors paying special attention to my heart, though the baby's strong movements seemed to mock their earlier concerns about my ability to carry a child.

When labor finally began, it was Grammy and Bapa who mobilized like a military operation of their own. They moved into that motel near the hospital, refusing to return home until they knew both mother and baby were safe. Their dedication was remarkable and would serve as a guide for my future self - here was the family support I'd missed in those early California years, now showing up in full force when I needed it most.

Looking back now, the mathematics of those dates tells its own story - a December 7th wedding and a June 3rd birth speaks plainly of a romance that didn't wait for wedding bells. But 1954 was a different time, when such things weren't discussed openly. Grammy and Bapa's quick acceptance and unwavering support during my pregnancy speaks volumes about their character. Their concern wasn't with dates on a calendar but with the welfare of their soon-to-be grandchild and their young daughter-in-law.

That first baby arrived on June 3rd, 1955, less than six months after the wedding. If anyone at the Corona Naval Hospital was counting months on their fingers, they kept it to themselves. The military had its own way of handling such matters - efficiency over judgment, paperwork over gossip. Besides, in the post-war baby boom, young marriages and quick pregnancies weren't unusual, even if some came sooner than others. June 3, 1955 I gave birth to our Gemini first born, Deborah Suzanne Dobbins "Debbie".

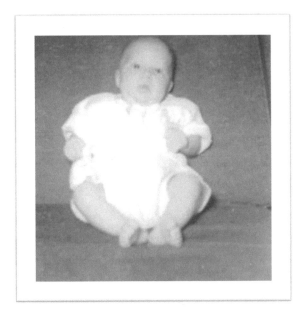

Debbie 2 months

Jerry managed to be there for the birth, a brief shore leave that seemed to pass in the blink of an eye. Then he was gone again, back to his minesweeper, leaving me to navigate new motherhood largely on my own. The other Navy wives, many with their own stories of rushed weddings and quick pregnancies, formed a protective circle around their newest member. In military life, you learned quickly not to judge - today's scandal was tomorrow's normal, and we all had our own versions of unconventional beginnings.

Those early weeks of motherhood were a blur of midnight feedings and daily discoveries. At eighteen, I was learning to be a mother while still barely grown myself. The monthly allotment from Jerry's Navy pay had to stretch to cover everything a growing family needed, and I quickly became an expert at budgeting. Every penny was accounted for - diapers, formula, and the endless list of baby necessities that seemed to multiply daily.

Just as I was getting my footing as a mother, learning the rhythms of life with a baby in military housing, life threw another surprise my way. My daughter wasn't even walking when I discovered I was pregnant again. The doctors who had once said I couldn't have children must have been shaking their heads somewhere - here I was, not only having babies, but having them in quick succession.

Managing a second pregnancy while caring for an infant brought new challenges. The military pay didn't stretch any further just because our family was growing faster than expected. Those months taught me creative budgeting skills that would serve me well through the years to come. I learned to sew out of necessity, making baby clothes and repurposing items while Jerry was at sea. The monthly allotment had to cover everything - there was no extra for store-bought luxuries.

Life on the base had its own rhythm. While other young wives my age were going to college or starting careers, I was mastering the art of washing diapers without a washing machine, hanging them on the line to dry in the California sun. The other Navy wives would joke that you could tell which families had infants by the rows of diapers fluttering like white flags of surrender in their backyards.

Our second daughter, Cynthia Lynn Dobbins, arrived May 17, 1957, marking another change in our growing family's life. Jerry's deployments meant he missed many of the daily moments - first steps, first words, the everyday miracles of watching our children grow. Letters and occasional photos had to bridge the gaps between his visits home. This was long before instant communication; a simple "I love you" had to travel across oceans by mail, often taking weeks to reach its destination.

The pattern was becoming clear - Jerry would come home on leave, we'd have precious few weeks together, and then he'd ship out again. Nine months later, give or take, another Dobbins would join the family, this time a son. We named him after Jerry's dad Donald (Bapa). Donald Glenn Dobbins was born December 15, 1959. It was almost mathematical in its precision, though nobody talked about it quite that directly. Grammy would just smile and start preparing for another grandchild, while I learned to navigate pregnancy and childbirth with an efficiency that came from practice.

The rhythm of my pregnancies tracked like a military schedule, each child arriving almost exactly two years after the last. My first born came on June 3, 1955. The second arrived May 17, 1957, the third on December 15, 1959, and my fourth - who would be my last, Laura Gay Dobbins - on February 23, 1961. Each pregnancy seemed to mark a different phase of Jerry's Naval career, our growing family keeping time like a well-calibrated clock.

Looking at these dates now, they tell a story of Jerry's leave patterns, of brief reunions between deployments that invariably led to another pregnancy. The military life had its own way of structuring our family planning - not through careful consideration, but through the scattered weeks when a sailor was home between sea duties. Each homecoming was precious, each goodbye marked by another life beginning.

The spacing of the children brought its own challenges and advantages. By the time my fourth was born in early 1960, I had children aged five, three, one, and newborn. While this meant multiple children in diapers - all cloth in those days, no modern disposables - it also meant they were close enough in age to be playmates. When you're essentially raising children alone while your husband is at sea, having them able to entertain each other is a blessing you learn to appreciate.

Managing these pregnancies while caring for young children required a kind of choreography that only military wives seemed to master. Each pregnancy found me a little more experienced, a little more prepared, but no less challenged by the logistics of caring for a growing brood largely on my own. The days were a constant juggle of nursing babies, changing diapers, and trying to give each child the attention they needed.

The timeline of my children's births reads like a military log: four children in five years, each arrival precisely timed two years apart. But behind these dates were the real stories - of carrying babies through hot California summers, of Grammy stepping in when the load became too heavy, of learning to be both mother and father during Jerry's long deployments.

The arrival of my fourth child in February 1960 marked not just the completion of our family, but the end of an era. The 1950s, with their rigid social structures and clear expectations for military wives, were giving way to a new decade. While the world was watching the Kennedy-Nixon debates and teenagers were dancing to new sounds on American Bandstand, I was mastering the logistics of managing four children under six years old.

The births of my children had spanned a remarkable period in American history. My first was born in 1955, when Rock Around the Clock was shocking parents and Rosa Parks was refusing to give up her bus seat. By the time my fourth arrived in 1960, America was on the cusp of tremendous social change. The predictable patterns of the 1950s - where a military wife knew exactly what was expected of her - were about to give way to something entirely different.

Jerry's transition out of the Navy brought its own changes. After years of calculating our lives around deployments and homecomings, we were suddenly facing civilian life. He took a job at Thrifty's Drug Store (now RiteAid), marking the beginning of a new chapter for our family. The military housing that had been our home, the community of Navy wives who had been my support system - all of this would soon be replaced by something new.

My twenties had been defined by pregnancy, childbirth, and early motherhood. While other women my age were just beginning to think about starting families, I had completed mine before my twenty-fifth birthday. The experiences had aged me in some ways, but they had also given me a kind of confidence that only comes from facing and overcoming continuous challenges.

Chapter 4

THE BUSY YEARS OF MOTHERHOOD

As the new decade dawned, I found myself standing at another threshold. The young girl who had once paraded down Main Street in a fluorescent shirt was now a mother of four, ready to begin yet another transformation. The 1960s would bring opportunities I couldn't have imagined during those long nights of nursing babies and waiting for letters from sea. The skills I'd learned as a military wife - resourcefulness, independence, the ability to manage on my own - were about to find new outlets in ways I never expected.

The 1960s arrived with the same explosive energy as my four young children racing through our house. While John F. Kennedy was promising a New Frontier for America, I was blazing my own trail - managing a household of six on a Thrifty Drug Store salary while looking for ways to contribute more than just motherhood to our family's future. The transition from military to civilian life brought its own challenges, but those years as a Navy wife had taught me something crucial: I could handle whatever life threw at me.

Our first big move was from Naval Housing in San Pedro to Duarte in the San Gabriel Valley of California. Back then the San Gabriel Valley was lush full of orange groves and rural living. It had a Father Knows Best vibe but instead of black and white television show, it was lush and fertile.

Our move to Duarte coincided with the nation's growing pains. The evening news (what little there was at that time) was filled with civil rights marches and space race developments all while I was orchestrating the daily parade of school lunches, homework supervision, and endless loads of laundry. We weren't just changing addresses; we were changing lifestyles. The military's structured environment, with its clear rules and support systems, gave way to the more fluid civilian world where you had to create your own structure and create it we did in our own way.

The house in Duarte became our first real home after years of military housing. It was nothing fancy, but it was ours - well at least, we were paying rent on it. While other mothers might have been content with the traditional role of homemaker, I found myself looking for more. Not because being a mother wasn't enough - those four children were my pride and joy - but because something in me had always pushed against accepted limitations. Something in me together with Jerry was craving the American Dream and we began the journey of buying our first home with 4 kids and one salary. Yes you could do that back then.

This marked our first real stake in the American Dream - a house we were buying, not renting. It was the early 1960s, and like many families, we were riding the wave of post-war prosperity into home ownership. While the Beach Boys were singing about California girls and surfing, we were creating our own California story in a modest house that somehow managed to contain our family of six.

There were some crazy moments during our life in Azusa. A very unique name for a city which would be taught my children to spell by the phrase, A-Z in the USA. We were truly living the American Dream and little did I realize I would become an advocate for not only the American Dream but everything that represented those freedoms and rights.

Everyone remembers where they were the day President Kennedy was assassinated in 1963. I do. Two of the kids were in school at Gladstone School in Azusa and the news shook the nation. The world seemed to stop turning for a moment. That day marked more than just a national tragedy; it symbolized the end of innocence for many Americans. For me, it marked a period of deeper reflection about what one person could contribute to their community, their family, and their own future. My path was about to be paved and I didn't even know it.

It was time for me to make an impact. Not in politics but as the "Paper Lady". That would be only one of my monikers through my life. Paper Lady was a "nick name" I was given because I delivered newspapers in bulk to "paper boys" to then deliver to their customers on their bikes.

Being the "Paper Lady" was unlike anything you'd see today. A little more obscure than rotary phones in today's world. We lived in an era before digital news and morning TV shows and newspapers were the lifeblood of information. Getting newspapers from the printing press to people's doorsteps was a complex operation and much more laborious than anything you might imagine being born in the last 20 years. I became a crucial link in this chain - I bridged the gap between the printing press and the young paper boys who would ultimately deliver the newspapers to individual homes.

Every afternoon, I'd load the family station wagon with hundreds of newspapers, bundled and tied with twine, fresh from the printing press. The weight of these bundles would make the car sag noticeably. My role was to ensure these papers reached the paper boys on time, in all weather conditions - rain, shine, or on those rare Southern California days when the elements weren't cooperative. News couldn't wait for good weather; people expected their papers regardless of conditions. I came to dread days of rain. The old song "It Never Rains in California" was only true until it wasn't. Ink stained hands from the freshly printed presses was not an option on those days.

Despite the sometimes inclement weather conditions, I became more than just a delivery person. To these paper boys, many of whom were barely older than my own children, I became a sort of surrogate mother. They were young entrepreneurs in their own right, learning responsibility and business skills through their paper routes. I made sure they got their papers on time, but I also kept an eye on them, offered encouragement, and sometimes served as a sounding board for their troubles.

The job of Paper Lady fit my family life perfectly. Often, my own children would ride along in the station wagon, turning what could have been just a job into a family adventure. We'd make our rounds, delivering bundles to predetermined spots where the paper boys would collect them. These young boys would then transform the flat papers into tight rolls, stuff them into their bicycle baskets or bags, and head out on their own routes through the neighborhoods.

My decision to become the "Paper Lady" came from that same spirit of independence that had served me so well as a military wife. The job wasn't glamorous - delivering papers to paperboys who would then deliver them to homes - but it offered something precious: flexibility to earn money while still being there for my children. In hindsight the modeling of being my own entrepreneur could be the reason my own kids have become entrepreneurs themselves. Something as simple as loading up the station wagon with bundles of newspapers, often with kids in tow, was my way of creating my own small business model before women were expected to do such things.

The early 1960s were a time of profound change in America. The Civil Rights movement was gaining momentum, the Cold War was intensifying, and women were beginning to question their traditional roles. While Betty Friedan was writing "The Feminine Mystique," I was quietly forging my own path to independence. As women we don't need a leader to be a leader in our own right. The paper route might have seemed like just a job to others, but it was really my first step toward something bigger - a way to contribute to our family's finances while maintaining the flexibility my children needed AND the training ground for my next adventures.

Our house in Azusa became more than just a home; it was a base of operations. I managed the paper route, cared for four active children, and still found time to take in other people's children for babysitting. These weren't conscious acts of feminism - we didn't use such terms then - they were simply what needed to be done. Jerry was building his career at Thrifty's, and I was building something of my own, though I wasn't quite sure what it was yet.

The early 1960s painted our daily routine in vivid colors. As headlines about the Space Race and Civil Rights movement rolled off the presses, I was teaching young entrepreneurs their first lessons in responsibility. These paper boys weren't just delivering news; they were learning life lessons about commitment, hard work, and the value of showing up every day, rain or shine. In my own way, I was shaping the next generation while still tending to my own growing brood. They were learning by example as well.

As I look back, those afternoon paper runs became a symphony of sorts - the creak of the station wagon's springs under the weight of fresh newsprint, the snap of twine as bundles were lifted, the chatter of young boys eager to begin their routes. While the rest of America was watching "Leave it to Beaver" and imagining the perfect suburban housewife, I was creating my own version of the American dream from behind the wheel of an overloaded station wagon.

Our family station wagon became a mobile command center of sorts. Command Centers would become an overriding theme in my life I would learn later. The kids would pile in after school, homework and snacks in tow, as we made our rounds through the neighborhoods of Azusa. We'd see the community through a unique lens - which houses had their lights on early, which streets were filling with playing children, which paper boys were having a tough day and needed an extra word of encouragement.

The paper route brought its own kind of freedom. While other mothers were confined to kitchen and diaper duties, I was building relationships throughout the community, learning the rhythm of neighborhoods, understanding the intricate dance of commerce and communication that kept our little corner of the world informed. The modest income it provided was important, but the independence it offered was priceless.

Those afternoon runs taught me something crucial about community - how news and information bound us together, how young boys could learn responsibility through the simple act of delivering papers, and how a mother of four could carve out her own unique place in the working world while still being there for her children. Little did I know then that this first taste of independence would lead to even greater adventures in the years to come.

As I look back, the news I helped deliver in those years told the story of an America in transformation. It was no FOX News, but it was what we had back then. As Martin Luther King Jr. shared his dream in Washington, and Betty Friedan's books were tucked into handbags across the nation, I was witnessing my own quiet revolution through the windows of that station wagon. Each bundle of papers represented not just news, but possibility - the possibility that a woman could be both mother and breadwinner, both nurturer and entrepreneur, that our country was the most incredible place on earth and I wanted to be integral in its development.

My paper boys, as I came to think of them, brought their own stories to our daily encounters. Some came from families where every penny of their paper route money went to helping at home. Others were saving for bikes or college dreams. In them, I saw echoes of my own childhood determination, that spark of independence that had carried me from Denver to California, through military wifehood, and now into this new chapter of life.

The route became a family affair. My children learned early that work wasn't something that happened in some distant office - it was immediate, tangible, and sometimes came with ink-stained hands. They watched as I managed accounts, handled complaints, and encouraged young boys to take pride in their work. These weren't lessons you could teach from a kitchen; they had to be lived. And so they were. Each of my children has forged a path of independence, love of country and entrepreneurship not to mention the American Dream.

As our family station wagon, much like a covered wagon, wound through the streets of Azusa each day, I began to see the community differently. Behind each door where a paper would land was a family connecting to the wider world through those ink-smudged pages. The Cuban Missile Crisis, the Beatles' arrival in America, the tragedy of JFK's assassination - these weren't just headlines we were delivering, but moments that bound our community together in shared experience.

The paper route offered something else too - a window into how communities function, how information flows, how people connect. These insights would prove invaluable in the years to come, though I couldn't have known it then. While I was simply trying to contribute to our family's income and maintain my independence, I was actually preparing for a future role in community organizing and political activism that would have seemed impossible in those ink-stained afternoons.

Our family station wagon was not just a portal into community, connection and entrepreneurship, but family togetherness. As a family we would pile in this old work horse for adventures that sometimes turned into misadventures. The early 1960s were the era of the great American road trip, when families would strike out on highways that weren't yet interstates, armed with paper maps and endless optimism. Our station wagon - the same one that faithfully carried newspapers during the week - became our passport to adventure on weekends and holidays.

Those early trips taught us about resilience in ways no planned vacation ever could. I remember one sweltering day when the station wagon broke down in the middle of the California desert. The temperature must have been well over 100 degrees, and there we were - four young children and their parents, watching heat waves dance over the hood of our stranded car. No cell phones, no AAA to call on a moment's notice. Just passing truckers and the kindness of strangers. These weren't the kind of family memories I'd planned to make, but they turned out to be the ones that stuck. My kids still remember them and I don't think I could have planned for a more poignant experience of family unity.

Keeping the family together meant more than just sharing a home - it meant sharing experiences, even when those experiences involved overheated radiators and roadside picnics. While other families might have opted for easier paths, we found our strength in these challenges. The children learned that breakdowns weren't disasters; they were just part of the adventure. They watched as their father tinkered with the engine, as their mother turned roadside stops into impromptu picnic adventures.

These station wagon days laid the foundation for what our family would become. When the temperature soared and tempers could have flared, we learned to find humor in our situations. When money was too tight for hotels, we discovered that sleeping under the stars could be its own kind of luxury. These weren't just trips; they were lessons in adaptability, in finding joy despite circumstances, in making memories out of mishaps.

Camping

Camping

Camping

As the 1960's began to crest, we had created enough for a downpayment with two incomes and make a big leap and moved to another San Gabriel Valley community. We moved to Covina, CA in 1964 which marked more than just a change of address - it represented a shift in our family's trajectory. This house on 5020 Nearglen in Covina, CA was a 4 bedroom, 2 bath and for a military family who scraped by with every penny, this home felt like a mansion. It was so much bigger than our Azusa home, with a spacious back room and a master bedroom that seemed palatial compared to what we'd known before. But more importantly, it offered opportunities for involvement in the community that would shape the next phase of my life.

While I continued to be the "paper lady," delivering bundles to my paper boys, I found myself drawn into school activities through the PTA. The garage that once held only newspapers soon became a storehouse for carnival prizes, and a mimeograph machine churning out flyers and announcements. The mimeograph became as familiar to me as my sewing machine. Those carnival preparations were massive undertakings - buying candy necklaces, selecting prizes, and organizing the goldfish bowl games where, inevitably, few fish survived their journey home.

We had begun our tent camping years with the station wagon which taught us resilience and resourcefulness and we were about to discover how a camper and moving to Covina felt like luxury, though still basic by today's standards.

Our station wagon adventures, with all their breakdowns and unexpected stops, eventually convinced us that we needed something more reliable for family travel. We finally had two incomes and it was an easy decision to buy a camper. It wasn't just about vacation comfort - it was about investing in our family's unity. While other families in the early 1960s were spending their money on modern appliances or new television sets, we chose to invest in experiences. Nobody had motorhomes back then; most people had campers you could walk through, but we got the one with the window between the cab and the back - which meant we couldn't hear the children when they held up their desperate signs reading "Help" or "Going to sleep."

The transition from station wagon to camper marked a new era in our family adventures. That same eighty dollars that bought our grocery basics at home could now stretch to cover two weeks of camping supplies. There was something liberating about packing up the camper, knowing we carried everything we needed with us. The children might have been living through the dawn of the space age, watching rockets launch on TV, but our family was having our own kind of adventures right here on Earth.

Despite the demands of the paper route and managing four young children, our family found ways to create adventures on a budget. The purchase of our first camper was a bold move for a family counting pennies, but it opened up a world of possibility. While other families might vacation at Disneyland or fashionable hotels, we discovered the freedom of the open road and the joy of camping - even with two children still in diapers.

Of course, camping with four young children wasn't exactly what you'd call a vacation - at least not for me, whether we were tent camping or camper camping, I still had littles in diapers. While other mothers might have been reading Ladies' Home Journal by their backyard pools, I was heating water on a Coleman stove to wash cloth diapers, hanging them to dry on a makeshift clothes line in Kings Canyon California. Looking back now, I wonder where I found the energy, but youth and determination can fuel seemingly impossible tasks.

These weren't just vacations; they were exercises in family unity and problem-solving. When bears would raid our campsite at Kings Canyon, or when the weather would turn unexpectedly harsh, we learned to face challenges together. I remember one particular night when a bear tried to come into our tent - we could only holler and make noise, hoping it would choose easier pickings elsewhere. The children still talk about these adventures, though they probably don't remember the endless work of keeping everyone fed, clean, and safe in the wilderness.

We often joined forces with a family friends. Together, with our family friends Carl and Judy and their family, we created our own little caravan of adventure seekers. The children would explore the wilderness while we adults set up camp, and in the evenings, after the little ones were tucked into sleeping bags, we'd sit around the campfire sharing stories and dreams and yes beer! These weren't just camping trips; they were building blocks of friendship and family bonds that would last a lifetime. The camper itself became a sort of mobile classroom for our children. While their classmates might learn about California geography from textbooks, our kids were experiencing it firsthand.

We loved heading out with our dear friends to places like Red Rock Canyon, Kings Canyon, Mammoth where the nights were cold and the stars seemed close enough to touch. The adults would sit around the campfire after the children were asleep, sharing stories and dreams while the desert wind whispered through the Joshua trees.

Thanksgiving became our traditional time at Red Rock Canyon, despite the freezing temperatures. While other families gathered around formal dining tables, we'd be huddled in our camper or around a campfire, celebrating in our own way. The children might have been cold, but they were creating memories that would last a lifetime.

As we settled into our forever family home in Covina, I became more and more involved in PTA. The PTA meetings in our Covina years became more than just school updates - they were my introduction to organized activism. While the nation was witnessing the rise of various movements for change, I was learning the grassroots basics of community organizing in the school multipurpose room. That mimeograph machine in our garage wasn't just printing carnival announcements; it was teaching me about communication, about reaching people, about making things happen.

I never imagined school carnivals required a kind of orchestration that would come naturally to me after years of managing four children and a paper route. While other mothers might volunteer for a single booth or bake sale, I found myself taking on more and more responsibility. The skills I'd developed - organizing, budgeting, managing multiple tasks - found new outlets in these community activities.

Our house on Nearglen became a hub of activity. The formal living room, furnished with an entertainment center that stretched across one wall and played Johnny Mathis records on Saturday mornings was the official "living room for company". It was mostly untouched as a shrine to suburban respectability. But the den and garage buzzed with constant motion. Carnival prizes were sorted and stored, committees met around our kitchen table, and plans were hatched for school events that grew more ambitious with each passing year.

The carnivals themselves were massive productions. I'd find myself shopping for prizes at Smart & Final, calculating how many goldfish we'd need (always accounting for the inevitable casualties), and organizing volunteers with the precision of a military campaign. Those years of managing a household on a strict budget had taught me how to stretch resources, how to make something from nothing, how to turn limited funds into maximum impact.

The experience of running these events showed me something crucial about myself - I had a knack for organization, for seeing the big picture while managing the smallest details. While other volunteers might focus on a single booth or task, I found myself naturally taking on more, coordinating multiple aspects, seeing how all the pieces fit together. This ability to orchestrate complex events while keeping track of countless details would serve me well in the years to come.

These were also the years when I discovered that leadership didn't always mean being the loudest voice in the room. Sometimes it meant being the person who showed up early to set up chairs, who stayed late to clean up, who remembered to thank the volunteers and make them feel valued. While Betty Friedan was writing about the "problem that has no name," I was quietly discovering my own path to fulfillment through community involvement and organizational leadership.

While my garage was filling with carnival prizes and the mimeograph machine was humming, the world outside our Covina home was changing dramatically. The mid-1960s brought upheaval across America - civil rights marches, anti-war protests, women beginning to question their traditional roles. But my own quiet revolution was happening in PTA meetings and school committee rooms, where I was learning the art of bringing people together for a common cause.

This led our den in our Covina home to become an unofficial campaign headquarters of sorts, though I didn't recognize it as such at the time. While organizing school carnivals and fundraisers, I was actually mastering the basics of what would later serve me in political organizing - budgeting, volunteer coordination, event planning, and perhaps most importantly, the ability to motivate people to give their time and energy to a shared goal.

It was during these years that I met Sam Otter, who would later draw me into local Republican politics. The skills I'd developed managing school events translated surprisingly well into political organizing. After all, what was a political campaign but a larger version of what I'd been doing - organizing people, managing resources, working toward a specific goal? The confidence I'd gained running school carnivals and managing PTA events gave me the foundation to step into this new arena.

My children watched as our home transformed into a center of activity. The back room that had once echoed with just family noise now hosted committee meetings and planning sessions. The dining table became a workspace where volunteers would gather, sharing coffee and ideas. Even the formal living room, with its entertainment center and Johnny Mathis records, occasionally served as a reception area for more official gatherings.

What set me apart, perhaps, was my willingness to take on any task, no matter how small or unglamorous. Whether it was stuffing envelopes, making phone calls, or organizing volunteers, I approached each job with the same determination I'd learned as a military wife and young mother. This wasn't about seeking attention or recognition; it was about getting things done, about making a difference in my community.

By the late 1960s, our Covina home had become more than just a family residence - it was a launching pad for increasingly broader community involvement. The organizational skills honed through PTA and school carnivals were about to find new purpose. While the world was watching man walk on the moon in 1969, I was taking my own small steps toward a bigger role in public service.

Life on Nearglen in the mid-1960s epitomized the American Dream - at least on the surface. Our block could have been a set for "Leave it to Beaver," with its neatly trimmed lawns and children playing freely in the streets. It was here that I found a friendship that would prove to be one of life's precious gifts - Alice Simples, who lived across the street with her husband Jim and their children, Linda, Gayla and Darla.

Alice and I formed a bond that went deeper than mere neighborhood friendship. Her daughter Gayla's had a medical condition with daily occurrence of seizures. This required round-the-clock attention and she showed me a different kind of maternal strength. While I was juggling my four active children, Alice was providing unwavering care for Gayla, teaching me about a depth of love and dedication I hadn't known existed. Our coffee conversations across kitchen tables became anchors in both our lives, moments of shared understanding and mutual support.

The paper route gradually wound down as our lives settled into new rhythms. Jerry's work at Thrifty's meant missed holidays and irregular hours - retail never sleeps, especially during the Christmas season. When he transitioned to becoming a sales rep for a resin company, the longer hours and increased travel brought new challenges to our family dynamic. The steady paycheck was welcome, but the cost was high - not just in his absence, but in the way the pressure of the job drove him to drink more frequently.

Once again, I found myself essentially functioning as a single mother, though this time by circumstance rather than military necessity. The stability we'd sought in moving to Covina had its own kind of instability. While our house on Nearglen provided the space our growing family needed, the empty chair at dinner became a more frequent sight. The camping trips continued - our family's attempt to hold onto togetherness - but even these couldn't mask the growing fissures in our family's foundation.

Our close friendships with other families, particularly the Simples, helped fill the gaps. Weekend barbecues, shared holidays, children running between houses - these created a sense of extended family that helped offset Jerry's increasing absences. The neighborhood itself became a kind of safety net, with its predictable rhythms and shared values. Yet beneath this veneer of suburban perfection, change was brewing - both in our family and in the larger world.

The mid-1960s brought more than just domestic changes - they marked my first real steps into political activism. Barry Goldwater's campaign in 1964 ignited something in me that had perhaps been smoldering since those early days of independence as a military wife. Sam Otter, who ran the Republican precincts in Covina, introduced me to the world of precinct walking. While other housewives might have been watching "As the World Turns," I was literally "turning" my world by walking neighborhoods, knocking on doors, and discovering a passion for grassroots political action.

I even managed to rope Jerry into volunteering, though politics wasn't naturally his thing. He'd come along, perhaps more out of loyalty than conviction, but his presence showed our children something important - that marriage was about supporting each other's interests, even if they weren't your own. This period of shared political activity gave us common ground during a time when other aspects of our marriage were showing strain.

The 1967 campaign for Ronald Reagan as Governor of California took my political involvement to a new level. Here was someone who spoke to the values I believed in, and I threw myself into the campaign with the same energy I'd once devoted to managing military life with four small children. The campaign headquarters in downtown Covina became my second home, much like the PTA office had been earlier.

Meanwhile, our children were growing into teenagers, asserting their own independence just as I was discovering mine. Their increasing self-sufficiency seemed to give me permission to expand my horizons beyond our Nearglen

Street home. Jerry's transition to the resin company in the late 1960s, with its demands for travel and longer hours, coincided with this period of change. His absences, while challenging for our family life, created space for me to develop my own interests and activities outside the home.

Chapter 5

DISCOVERING A PASSION FOR POLITICS

The contrast between my growing political activism and the traditional suburban life we'd built was striking. While I was organizing campaign events and walking precincts, our home was still the site of family barbecues and neighborhood gatherings. The camping trips continued, though now they felt more precious - attempts to hold onto family cohesion in a time of increasing independence for all of us.

Our house on Nearglen reflected these changes. The garage that had once stored only carnival prizes and camping gear now held campaign materials and voter lists. The dining room table that had hosted so many family dinners became the site of campaign strategy sessions. Even our family camping trips took on new dimensions - political discussions around the campfire replaced simple storytelling, as current events and social changes couldn't help but seep into our family time.

The children, growing into their teenage years, watched their mother transform from "the paper lady" into something else entirely. They saw how community involvement could lead to bigger things, how saying "yes" to one small volunteer opportunity could open doors to larger purposes. Perhaps most importantly, they witnessed a woman of their mother's generation refusing to be limited by traditional roles, even while maintaining her commitment to family

Politics found me through that simple encounter on Cienega Street with Sam Otter. Sam managed the Republican precincts in our area and would become the catalyst for a whole new chapter in my life. When he asked if I could help with walking precincts and talking to people, I said "sure" - that simple word would change the trajectory of my life in ways I couldn't have imagined.

The 1964 Goldwater campaign became my political baptism. While the nation was watching the Beatles on Ed Sullivan and dealing with mounting tensions over civil rights, I was discovering the grassroots essence of American democracy. Walking precincts wasn't just about delivering campaign materials - it was about connecting with people, understanding their concerns, and learning how government touched everyday lives. The skills I'd developed as the "paper lady" translated perfectly - organizing routes, managing volunteers, keeping track of who had been contacted and who hadn't.

My involvement grew as I met more couples and families through these political activities. The Republican headquarters in downtown Covina became a second home, much like the PTA office had been. But this was different - this wasn't about organizing school carnivals anymore. This was about shaping the future of our community, our state, and our nation. So many different people began to come into our lives, including the The Burgers who owned a large estate in the Covina Hills. Their annual Republican barbecues, introduced me to a network of like-minded people who saw politics as a way to make real change.

By the time Ronald Reagan ran for governor in 1967, I was fully immersed in the world of politics. Reagan sparked something in the community - and in me - that went beyond typical campaign enthusiasm. His message resonated with the values I'd developed through years of managing family, work, and community involvement. I threw myself into organizing events, managing volunteers, and creating the kind of grassroots support that would help carry him to victory.

The late 1960s saw my political involvement deepen from simple volunteer to trusted organizer. While other housewives might have been watching "Dark Shadows" in the afternoons, I was at Republican headquarters, learning the intricacies of campaign organization. The headquarters had its own energy - a mix of idealism and practical action that suited my natural inclinations perfectly. We weren't just talking about change; we were working to make it happen.

The San Gabriel Valley Republican Women's Club became another cornerstone of my political education. This wasn't just about tea parties and social gatherings - these women were serious about politics and policy. When I was selected as a delegate to go to Washington D.C. for a Republican Women's Conference, it marked a significant milestone.

April 14, 1969, found me bound for Washington D.C. for the Republican Women's Conference - a far cry from my paper delivery days. That trip, documented in local papers with photos of carefully packed suitcases and eager faces, marked a turning point. I wasn't just a local volunteer anymore; I was becoming a recognized force in Republican politics. Mrs. Walter Burgers, President of the East San Gabriel Valley Republican Women's Club, supervised our packing, but what she was really overseeing was my transition from local activist to broader political engagement.

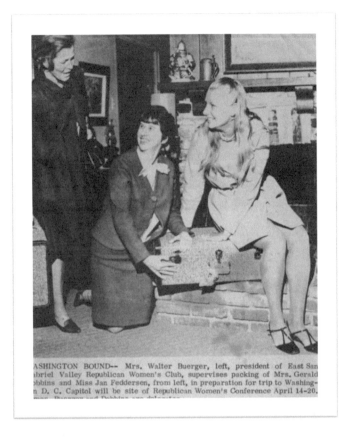

ASHINGTON BOUND-- Mrs. Walter Buerger, left, president of East San
abriel Valley Republican Women's Club, supervises packing of Mrs. Gerald
obbins and Miss Jan Feddersen, from left, in preparation for trip to Washing-
n D. C. Capitol will be site of Republican Women's Conference April 14-20.

Peggy Goes to Washington

The Burgers' annual barbecues at their hillside estate became more than just social gatherings - they were political networking events that helped me understand the broader scope of party politics. Dr. Burger, respected in the community, opened doors to relationships that would prove valuable in years to come. These events taught me something crucial about politics - that personal connections and trust were as important as policy positions.

My natural organizational abilities found perfect expression in political work. Whether it was organizing precinct walks, managing phone banks, or coordinating campaign events, I approached each task with the same attention to detail that had served me well in managing a household of six. The skills learned from organizing school carnivals translated perfectly to political rallies - it was all about managing people, resources, and timing.

Betty Burgers' Women's Republican Club meetings became a regular part of my life. We hosted bingo nights and other fundraising events, but these weren't just social gatherings - they were opportunities to build the kind of grassroots support that could change election outcomes. I learned that politics wasn't just about big speeches and campaign promises; it was about the patient work of building relationships and trust within the community.

What set me apart wasn't just willingness to work - plenty of people were willing to work. It was my ability to see a project through from beginning to end, to handle both the big picture and the smallest details. When other volunteers might focus on a single task, I saw how all the pieces fit together. Campaign headquarters under my organization ran like well-oiled machines, with every volunteer's talents put to best use.

I developed a reputation for finding creative solutions to campaign challenges. When traditional fundraising fell short, I'd organize events that brought in both money and new supporters. The bingo nights at Republican headquarters became legendary, not just for the funds they raised but for the community they built. People came for the games but stayed for the political engagement - exactly as I'd planned.

My approach to political organizing wasn't about following a rulebook - it was about getting results. Just as I'd found ways to manage a paper route while raising four children, I found ways to make political campaigns work despite limited resources. When we needed campaign materials but had a tight budget, I learned to make our own. Eventually, I even bought a button-making machine, creating custom campaign buttons that became sought-after items at political events.

The late 1960s saw me taking on increasingly responsible roles in campaign organization. I wasn't just walking precincts anymore - I was designing walking strategies, mapping out neighborhoods, and training other volunteers. My kitchen table often disappeared under maps and voter lists, while the garage stored an ever-growing collection of campaign materials. The kids learned to answer phones with proper campaign etiquette - they were getting their own education in civic engagement, whether they wanted it or not.

By the end of the 1960s, my political organizing had given me something invaluable - a reputation for getting things done, no matter the obstacles. When others saw problems, I saw logistics to be managed. When they saw impossible deadlines, I saw schedules to be orchestrated. This reputation extended beyond party circles into the broader community. I had developed a network that ranged from precinct workers to political candidates, from community leaders to party officials.

The skills I'd honed organizing Republican events translated perfectly into what would come next. Managing volunteers, coordinating complex schedules, handling sensitive information, and most importantly, understanding how to work with people from all walks of life - these were exactly the qualities needed for the upcoming 1970 decennial census.

When the Census Bureau started looking for people who could manage large-scale operations and handle detailed information gathering, my political organizing experience made me a natural fit. They needed someone who could train and supervise others, someone who understood the importance of accurate data collection, someone who could navigate both government requirements and community relationships. Without realizing it, my years of political activism had been preparing me for this next chapter.

The transition from political volunteer to government worker might have seemed unusual to some, but to me, it was a natural progression. Both roles required the same fundamental skills - organizing people, managing information, and getting results. As the 1970s dawned, I was ready to take these abilities into a new arena, one that would challenge me in ways I hadn't expected and open doors I hadn't imagined.

By the time the Census Bureau opportunity arose in 1970, I was more than ready for the next step. The skills I'd developed through political volunteering, community organizing, and yes, even managing four children and a paper route, had prepared me for this move into professional public service. The timing seemed perfect - the children were more independent, Jerry's work kept him traveling, and I had discovered a passion for community involvement that needed a bigger outlet.

The year 1970 marked more than just the start of a new decade - it marked my entry into government service through the Census Bureau. While others might have seen it as just a job, I approached it with the same independent spirit that had characterized my paper route days. The government might have had its rules and regulations, but I had my own way of getting things done.

What started as simply volunteering for the decennial census evolved into something far more significant. The Census Bureau, with all its bureaucratic structures, became my training ground for navigating government systems while maintaining my own approach to problem-solving. When other workers might give up on hard-to-reach respondents, I'd be out at 9 or 10 o'clock at night, waiting for a highway patrol officer to return home so I could complete an interview. I'd venture into neighborhoods others avoided, understanding that every person counted - literally and figuratively.

This period also introduced me to Tom Mew who would become my second husband, though that was still sometime in the future. We worked together supervising others, managing the office, and conducting tests for new hires. The Census Bureau became more than just a workplace - it was a community of its own, with its own dynamics and relationships. The office in downtown Los Angeles hummed with activity, and I found myself increasingly drawn into the world of government service.

Looking back on those years between 1965 and 1970, I can see how each experience built upon the last. From PTA meetings to political campaigns, from organizing school carnivals to managing campaign events, from raising children to raising awareness about political issues - each role prepared me for the next. The cracks appearing in our family's traditional structure weren't signs of breakdown but of transformation. We were all growing, changing, finding our own paths while trying to maintain the bonds that held us together.

The 1970s would bring even greater changes - professional opportunities, political involvement, and personal challenges that would test the foundation we'd built. But the lessons learned during these busy years of motherhood and community involvement would prove invaluable in the decades to come. The woman who had once delivered papers to support her family was about to deliver something else entirely - her own vision of what a woman could accomplish in public service.

Chapter 6

SECOND ACT IN PUBLIC SERVICE

The skills I'd developed managing school carnivals and paper routes were about to be put to much broader use. While the 1970s approached with their promise of social change and women's liberation, I was already charting my own course toward independence and public service.

The transition began almost accidentally in 1970 with the Census Bureau. They were asking for volunteers for the decennial census, and I raised my hand - something that had become almost second nature to me by then. This wasn't just about counting people; it was about understanding our community at its most fundamental level. Those early days of going door-to-door, asking questions about households and toilets, were giving me insights into our community that no amount of PTA meetings could provide. The Census Bureau work would prove to be just the beginning of a journey that would lead me from volunteer to professional, from community organizer to political activist.

The Census Bureau was gearing up for its decennial count of 1970 - a massive undertaking that happened only once every ten years. When they put out the call for volunteers for this special project, I raised my hand, just as I had for countless political and school events before. It seemed like a natural extension of the community work I'd been doing - after all, I knew the neighborhoods, understood how to talk to people, and had experience organizing large-scale efforts.

What I didn't know then was that this simple act of volunteering would open a door to an entirely new chapter in my life. The transition from political volunteer to government worker might have seemed unusual to some, but to me, it was a natural progression. Both roles required the same fundamental skills - organizing people, managing information, and getting results. My years of coordinating campaign volunteers, managing voter registrations, and handling sensitive political information had unknowingly prepared me for government service.

The Census Bureau quickly recognized something in my approach that set me apart. Perhaps it was the way I could organize teams efficiently, or how I wasn't afraid to go the extra mile to get accurate information. Maybe it was simply that I brought the same energy and dedication to this government work that I'd brought to political organizing. Whatever the reason, what started as volunteer work for the decennial census evolved into a job offer for ongoing census operations.

The 1970 Census wasn't just another government job - it was a perfect stage for someone who'd never quite fit into conventional boxes. While other census workers might stick to comfortable neighborhoods and daylight hours, I found myself driving into Los Angeles at 9 or 10 o'clock at night, waiting for a highway patrol officer to return from his shift just so I could complete an interview, and courageously canvasing neighborhoods that the normal worker would not go near. The Census Bureau wanted their numbers; I wanted them to be right.

Government work came with its own peculiar constraints, but I'd learned from my political organizing days that rules were often more flexible than they appeared. When they asked us to mark whether people we were testing were black or white, I questioned not just the legality but the logic of such requirements. The bureaucracy wanted simple categories in a world that was anything but simple. I found ways to work within the system while quietly challenging its limitations.

My approach to the job raised eyebrows among the more traditional government workers. When others might give up on hard-to-reach respondents, I'd venture into neighborhoods they avoided. Every person counted - literally and figuratively - and I was determined to get an accurate count, even if it meant unconventional methods. This wasn't just about fulfilling job requirements; it was about ensuring every community was properly represented.

The downtown Los Angeles federal building became my new base of operations, but I brought with me all the skills I'd developed organizing political campaigns. Managing teams of interviewers wasn't so different from coordinating precinct workers. Training new hires required the same patience and attention to detail I'd used in teaching volunteers how to walk neighborhoods. Even the paperwork, endless as it seemed, was just another form of the record-keeping I'd mastered in campaign headquarters.

What set me apart wasn't just willingness to work hard - plenty of people worked hard. It was my ability to see beyond the bureaucratic requirements to the real purpose of our work. When my young boss questioned my dedication to a project, suggesting I might leave before it was completed, I stood my ground. "I'm working on a project," the same thing I told Dick Mountjoy when he first offered me a job. "I can't leave until it's finished." That commitment to completing what I started, regardless of new opportunities, would become one of my defining characteristics.

What began as temporary work for the decennial census evolved into something more substantial. While other volunteers completed their assignments and moved on, I found myself drawn deeper into the Census Bureau's ongoing operations. The federal building downtown became my new territory, as different from my previous domains of PTA meetings and campaign headquarters as it could be, yet somehow familiar in its need for organization and efficiency.

The regular surveys that followed the big decennial count required a different kind of dedication. This wasn't just about counting heads anymore - it was about understanding communities, tracking employment patterns, and gathering the kind of detailed information that would shape government policy. I approached each survey as if it were a campaign, with the same attention to detail that had made me effective in political organizing.

My supervisors soon learned that I had my own way of doing things. When they assigned cases that others had given up on, I'd find creative ways to complete them. If a respondent worked night shifts, I'd be there when their shift ended. If someone was particularly hard to reach, I'd study their patterns and figure out the best time to catch them. The bureaucrats might raise their eyebrows at my methods, but they couldn't argue with my results.

The Law Enforcement Assistance Administration surveys became my specialty. Working with the Auditor Controller of Hawaii showed me how government operations extended far beyond my familiar San Gabriel Valley. These assignments required a delicate touch - dealing with sensitive information, understanding complex regulations, and maintaining confidentiality while still getting the necessary data.

But this new career was causing ripples at home. The hours weren't always predictable, and the travel took me away from family responsibilities more often. Jerry's own career as a sales rep kept him on the road frequently, and our paths seemed to cross less and less. The children were older now, more independent, but the dynamics of our family life were shifting in ways that would prove significant.

Success at the Census Bureau brought professional satisfaction, but it also meant longer hours and more responsibility. While I was proving myself in the professional world, managing complex surveys and supervising teams from our Covina office, my home life was showing increasing strain. Jerry's work with the resin company kept him traveling more, and when he was home, the drinking had become a serious issue. We were like ships passing in the night, each absorbed in our own worlds.

While I was finding my professional footing at the Census Bureau, my marriage to Jerry was unraveling. The signs had been there - his increased drinking, the growing distance between us, and finally, a confrontation that made it clear things had reached a breaking point. When he came home one night questioning where I'd been, my answer was simple and true: I'd been at work, and he could verify that with anyone at the office. His response threatening to "beat the crap" out of me. Sadly this revealed how far we'd fallen. My reply was equally direct: "If you beat on me, you gotta go to sleep sometime and you won't wake up." I walked away and went to bed, but we both knew something fundamental had shifted. I remember this so clearly because it was the final death blow to our marriage. I never give up on projects, but this one's expiration date had come due.

By 1974, our marriage of nearly twenty years had ended. The children were older - some already establishing their own lives - but divorce is never easy, especially after building a life together since my teenage years. The Census Bureau work became my lifeline during this transition, providing not just financial independence but a sense of purpose and identity separate from my role as wife and mother.

My divorce from Jerry was painful but necessary. The children were older now – Debbie already out of the house - but it still meant restructuring our entire family dynamic. The Census Bureau work became my anchor during this turbulent time. The structured nature of government work, the clear expectations and responsibilities, provided stability when my personal life felt anything but stable.

The following years were about rediscovering myself as an independent woman. The skills I'd developed managing surveys and supervising teams served me well in managing my new life. Tom Mew, a colleague at the Census Bureau, would enter the picture, and we married in 1976.

The marriage to Tom Mew seemed like a fresh start - two Census Bureau professionals who understood each other's world. But what appeared promising on the surface would reveal itself as another painful lesson in resilience. Tom's betrayal cut deep – he not only cheated on me, but raided my bank account which I had spent decades saving. Once again, I found myself facing the harsh reality that marriage didn't guarantee security.

But this time was different. The young woman who had once moved from motel to motel with her mother, who had managed as a military wife on a strict budget, who had raised four children while delivering newspapers - she had grown into someone who knew her own strength. When I discovered Tom's financial embezzlement and infidelity, I didn't just walk away - I fought back. Through legal action, I was awarded ownership of our home, a victory that helped me establish my own independence.

With the sale of that home, I purchased my own home in Monrovia, California. The late 1970s marked a turning point. This wasn't just any house - it was mine, bought with my own money, a testament to my ability to stand on my own. That house would become my home for the next 37 years, a symbol of the independence I'd fought so hard to achieve.

It was during this period of personal rebuilding that Dick Mountjoy entered the picture. In 1978, he sought me out, having heard about my organizational abilities and dedication to getting things done. His offer of a job would open the door to what would become the most politically active and professionally fulfilling period of my life. But true to my character, when he first approached me about working for him, my response was characteristic of my commitment to finishing what I started: I couldn't leave my Census Bureau job until the project I was working on was properly completed.

On an evening in 1978 Dick Mountjoy and his wife Arlene came to my house to discuss a job opportunity. They couldn't have known they were offering more than just a position - they were providing a platform where all my life experiences would converge. My response about needing to finish my Census Bureau project first must have surprised them. "A government employee that won't leave a project" became something of a running joke, but it spoke to the dedication that would characterize our entire working relationship.

The transition from Census Bureau to Mountjoy's office wasn't just a job change - it was stepping into my destiny. While I was initially hired as a secretary for his new Assembly office, I quickly made it clear that title wouldn't suffice. "People come in the front door, and when they see I'm the secretary, they ask to talk to somebody higher," I told Dick. "Just give me any other title - office manager, anything - so I can actually help these people instead of having them dismiss me."

What followed was a masterclass in political organization and constituent service. Doug Boyd was the official Chief of Staff in Dick's office and I was the "secretary". As Doug struggled with his personal demons, I became the office's driving force. When casework wasn't being followed up on, I did what I always do, brought in volunteers. It was at this moment, I recruited Dixie, Dodie, and Agnes who became life long friends. We took this Assembly office by storm. Even before personal computers were common place in businesses, I recognized the need for one in our offices. Once they were installed, I immediately recognized the potential for constituent outreach that others may have missed back then, something that is essential for all businesses in today's world. Every skill I'd developed - from managing paper routes to organizing political campaigns, from handling Census Bureau surveys to navigating government bureaucracy - found its purpose.

My role evolved far beyond any official title. I became Dick's right hand, his trusted advisor, and often his political conscience. Where others saw rules and regulations, I saw possibilities. When Willie Brown, then then Speaker of the Assembly in California, tried to control Dick's movements in Sacramento, I helped him orchestrate creative solutions. Once such time involved Willie forbidding members of the Assembly to leave Sacramento for the weekend. Instead Dick took Willie's car to the airport and caught a commercial plane home. These weren't just political maneuvers; they were expressions of the independence and resourcefulness I'd cultivated throughout my life.

The California Republican Assembly (CRA) became one of our most powerful tools for grassroots organizing. I helped establish it as a fundamental force in Republican politics, understanding that real political power comes from organized, committed groups rather than loose associations. We turned the

Arcadia Republican Headquarters into a model of efficiency and fundraising success, with regular events that brought in both money and supporters.

The bingo nights I helped organize at Arcadia headquarters became legendary - not just for the funds they raised, but for the community they built. Every detail mattered, from the scheduling to the prizes to making sure the right people were in the room. This wasn't just about raising money; it was about creating a network of committed supporters who would be there when we needed them.

Dick's ability to fly his own plane transformed our political reach. While other legislative staff might be constrained by commercial flight schedules, we could be anywhere in California on short notice. I remember flying home from Sacramento one particularly stormy night, watching ice form on the wings. Dick had always told me that if ice freezes on the outside of the plane, you're going down. When I pointed out the ice building up, he just said, "Don't worry about it. I got it covered. I have a defroster." But the ice kept building, and my concern grew until he had to make an emergency landing - ostensibly so I could use the bathroom, but really to calm my nerves.

Those flights between Sacramento and the district weren't just travel time - they were strategy sessions. While Dick piloted the plane, we'd discuss legislation, plan events, or strategize about upcoming votes. The flexibility of private aviation meant we could maintain a presence both in the district and at the Capitol, crucial for building and maintaining political influence.

Fund-raising events under my organization became more than just political necessities - they were community celebrations. I understood that successful fundraising wasn't just about asking for money; it was about making people feel part of something important. Whether it was organizing a major dinner event or coordinating intimate gatherings with key supporters, every detail was carefully planned and executed.

My role with Dick evolved far beyond typical staff responsibilities. When Dick co-authored Proposition 187 in 1994, a ballot initiative to establish a state-run citizenship screening system and prohibit illegal immigrants from using non-emergency health care, public education, and other services in California, this was not just about managing office responses - I was helping shape strategy. The initiative demanded someone who understood both government operations and grassroots organizing, skills I'd spent decades honing. During the late 1980s and early 1990s, our office became a focal point for conservative activism in California. The same issues that recently re-elected Donald Trump as the 47th President of our United States were calling me decades earlier.

One of my proudest achievements was developing a comprehensive constituent services operation. We created a computer database of district residents long before these type of technological things were common, allowing us to send personalized letters to constituents about issues that mattered to them. Willie Brown might have controlled the Assembly, but in our district, we controlled the truthful flow of information and assistance to our constituents.

When Dick simultaneously won election to both the Assembly and Senate seats - something that wasn't supposed to be possible - it was my organizational skills that helped navigate the unprecedented situation. He chose to remain in the Assembly to try to remove Willie Brown as Speaker, and I managed the complex political choreography this required. Our office became known as the place where impossible things happened regularly.

The relationships I built during these years extended far beyond our district. Republican leaders throughout California knew that if they needed something done - really done, not just talked about - I was the person to call. Whether it was organizing a statewide event, coordinating multiple campaign offices, or managing complex political negotiations, my reputation for competence and discretion made me a trusted figure in state politics.

1984 Republican National Convention

By the mid-1990s, I had become more than just Dick's assistant - I was a political force in my own right. My house in Monrovia which represented my independence had become a kind of unofficial political salon, where strategy sessions and campaign planning often took place. But as the century drew to a close, I began thinking about adding new dimensions to my life. While politics would always be in my blood, the world was big, and there were places I wanted to see, things I wanted to experience.

Throughout my years of public service, travel had already become an integral part of my life, though initially it was mostly work-related. The Census Bureau had first sent me to Hawaii, where my dedication to getting accurate data led to the Auditor Controller offering his timeshare for my stay. Those early Hawaii trips taught me about adapting to new places and making the most of unexpected opportunities.

Republican conventions had taken me across the country, from Washington D.C. to various state capitals. I remember being at my first national convention when Bush Sr. was choosing a running mate, serving not as a delegate but in a special role that allowed me more freedom to move around and gather intelligence. I'd often find myself outside the press areas, picking up information that would prove valuable to our political operations back home.

Crisscrossing California with Dick in his plane had made me comfortable with travel in all its forms. From emergency landings due to ice on the wings to late-night flights back from Sacramento, I'd learned to take adventure in stride. These experiences, combined with my natural independence and organizational skills, had prepared me for broader horizons.

Dick's Jeeps

Dick, Planes

Chapter 7

TRAVEL AND NEW HORIZONS

The urge to explore had always been part of my nature, but it expressed itself differently through the seasons of my life. Travel had been woven into the fabric of my life from those early days of packing four kids into a station wagon held together by hope and prayer, setting out across the California desert with no guarantee we'd make it without a breakdown. We'd progressed from breakdown-prone road trips to family camping expeditions in our trusty camper. Each of these journeys, though challenging, planted seeds of confidence that would later bloom into much bigger adventures. The Census Bureau work had expanded my horizons to Hawaii, teaching me that work travel could open doors to new experiences.

Those family road trips taught me something crucial about travel - it wasn't just about reaching a destination, but about handling whatever came your way. When our station wagon would inevitably overheat in the middle of nowhere, with temperatures soaring past 100 degrees, we learned to turn mishaps into memories. The children watched as their parents problem-solved, adapted, and kept going. These weren't just vacations; they were life lessons in resilience.

The transition from our breakdown-prone station wagon to a proper camper marked our first step up in the travel world. Those camping trips became our version of family vacations, though others might have questioned the wisdom of camping with two children still in diapers. Having to heat water on a Coleman stove to wash cloth diapers might not sound like a vacation to most, but it taught me that with enough determination, you could make anything work.

As my political involvement grew, so did my travel horizons. Republican conventions took me to cities across America, each trip adding another layer to my understanding of how to move through the world. These weren't just political gatherings; they were opportunities to explore new places, to learn how different cities worked, to understand that the world was both bigger and more accessible than I'd once imagined.

Washington D.C. became a familiar destination through political conventions and women's Republican events. That first Republican Women's Conference in April 1969 was more than just a political gathering - it was my introduction to the capital's unique rhythm. While other attendees might stick to official functions, I learned to navigate the city like a local, discovering that the real pulse of politics often beat strongest in unexpected places.

The true adventures began when we ventured beyond official itineraries. I remember one particular trip with Dixie, a lifelong loyal volunteer at Dicks office, when we decided that seeing Washington wasn't enough - New York City beckoned. In those days, spontaneity ruled our travels. We drove down from D.C., undaunted by New York's reputation for being unwelcoming to tourists. The city was different then - grittier, more challenging, but also more authentic. We happened to arrive during the city's first gay pride parade, and instead of retreating to our hotel, we wove through the crowds, determined to experience everything the city had to offer.

Our New York adventure led us to the Windows on the World, atop the World Trade Center. We arrived after lunch service had ended, but weren't about to let that stop us from experiencing one of the world's most famous restaurants. "Can we get Bloody Marys?" we asked. The drinks came with the attendant celery stalk and we laughed as we joked, "Pretend it's salad." Standing there, sipping our drinks and looking out over Manhattan, we couldn't have imagined that this magnificent space would one day exist only in memory. The view from those windows taught me something about perspective - both literally and figuratively.

Looking down at the city from above, I understood that every street I'd found daunting from ground level was just part of a greater whole.

The city itself became our classroom. Times Square, Ellis Island, each neighborhood we explored added another layer to our understanding. At Ellis Island, I was struck by the stories of immigrants passing through its halls, the meticulous records kept of each arrival. This wasn't just history - it was a testament to how America had processed and documented its newest arrivals, so different from what we were seeing in our current times.

These domestic travels were teaching me invaluable lessons about adaptation and observation. Each city had its own character, its own unwritten rules. Learning to read these subtle signs, to navigate different urban environments with confidence, was preparing me for even bigger adventures to come. The woman who had once been intimidated by a move from Denver to California was now confidently exploring America's greatest cities, and my hunger for new experiences was only growing stronger.

The jump from domestic to international travel came through family connections, as many of life's biggest adventures often do. When my son Donnie and his wife Donna were stationed in Washington D.C., visiting them was still comfortably within my American travel experience. But when orders came for them to move to Yugoslavia, I faced a decision: would I let the Iron Curtain become a barrier to seeing my family? The answer, naturally, was no. The woman who had once driven across the desert with four small children wasn't about to let a little thing like international borders stop her.

Yugoslavia in those days wasn't a tourist destination - it was a Communist country where Western visitors were viewed with suspicion. Military families like Donnie and Donna's lived in a unique bubble, straddling the line between American and local life. Watching my grandchildren attend an international school, learning French and adapting to a completely different way of life, I saw how travel could transform not just the traveler but entire generations.

My time in Yugoslavia opened my eyes to a world of contrasts. While the military base maintained its American routines, step outside and you entered a different world entirely. The local markets operated on their own schedule - if you didn't get there early enough on market day, you simply went without. This wasn't like running to the grocery store back home; it was a lesson in how much of what we took for granted was really cultural luxury.

From Yugoslavia, we ventured into Italy, an adventure that involved loading our car onto a train - a completely foreign concept to someone used to American road trips. Italy proved to be both challenging and enlightening. The further we got from tourist areas, the less English we encountered. I remember ordering what I thought was a salad and getting octopus instead. These "mishaps" became part of the adventure, teaching me that the best travel stories often come from the unexpected.

One particularly memorable excursion had us driving around an Italian island. Coming around a curve, we encountered goats in the road. Dick, who was with us on this trip, suggested we feed them. What started as feeding two curious goats quickly evolved into a situation worthy of a comedy film as an entire herd appeared over the hill. These moments of unexpected joy, of plans derailed by local reality, became the hallmarks of true travel experience.

In politics, timing is everything. The same could be said for travel. As my role in Dick Mountjoy's office became well-established, my thoughts turned to exploring the broader world. My first venture into historical international travel came through the National Religious Broadcasters (NRB). An unlikely portal to my world travels. The NRB was a radio show hosted by Warren Duffy, everyone just called him "Duffy". As my life was always full of coincidences, I met Sandy Gray who also worked for Duffy, at a CRA meeting. Duffy was organizing a NRB sponsored trip to Ireland and the transition from family-centered travel to more purposeful exploration came naturally. My first international experiences had taught me valuable lessons about adaptation and expectation. This organized trip with Sandy would take us on all new adventures.

Sandy, who would become my dearest and most loyal friend worked for Duffy the organizer of these trips. Sandy emerged as my perfect travel companion. We shared not just rooms but a philosophy about travel - we weren't there just to see places, but to understand them, to dig deeper, quite literally, sometimes, into their history and meaning.

Ireland, with its connection to both the Dobbins family line and, coincidentally, the Mountjoy name, provided a perfect entry point into international travel beyond visiting my family. Discovering Mountjoy Square and Mountjoy Castle, felt like a delightful validation of the political world I inhabited back home. But what truly captured me about Ireland wasn't just the historical connections - it was the living, breathing country itself. I found myself mesmerized by the impossible-to-photograph green of the hills, a color so vibrant and unique that no camera could do it justice.

These early solo travels gave me confidence to venture further. When Sandy and I connected through our work - she with Duffy and I with Dick Mountjoy's office - we discovered we shared not just a work ethic but a curiosity about the world. Our first trips together helped us develop a rhythm, learning each other's travel styles and preferences.

Sandy and Peggy Travel Companions

Our trips to Greece became a regular part of our travel calendar, with each visit revealing new layers of this ancient land. Sometimes we'd find ourselves on small transport ships between islands, where accommodations were basic at best. I remember one time when Sandy and I were assigned a tiny cabin with bunk beds. "I can't sleep in the top bunk," I explained, "because I have to get up and go to the bathroom at night." Sandy, always adaptable, took the top bunk without complaint. These small negotiations between travel companions often meant the difference between a good trip and a great one.

Each trip was peeling back another layer of history and culture. We'd find ourselves where tourists rarely ventured. One particular island, with its white buildings and blue roofs against the azure sea, became a favorite. But we weren't content just to admire the views - we wanted to understand how people lived in these places, how ancient traditions survived in the modern world.

This deepening approach to travel prepared us for what would become our most meaningful journeys - the trips to Israel with NRB. Each visit revealed new aspects of both ancient and modern life, from the political complexities of contemporary Jerusalem to the archaeological sites that connected us to thousands of years of human history.

Israel had become a bucket list destination for me and when we finally ventured there, Israel revealed itself to us layer by layer. Quite literally in the case of the archaeological digs we participated in the stories woven into the fabric of this culture were awe inspiring. These weren't tourist experiences - we were down in the earth, carefully uncovering artifacts from ancient civilizations. Every jar, bottle, dish we uncovered told a story of daily life from thousands of years ago. As Sandy said, "I never cared about archaeology until we went to Israel." There's something profound about holding a piece of pottery that last saw sunlight when Jerusalem was still young.

The ancient cities we explored had been buried and rebuilt multiple times, each layer representing a different era. When invaders would come, they would simply level the existing city and build on top of it. We'd be down in these excavated cities, finding floors and rooms, chapels and living spaces, each telling its own story of life in biblical times. The experience transformed how we understood history - it wasn't just dates in a book anymore, but tangible, touchable reality.

Modern Israel impressed us just as much as its ancient sites. The country had mastered desert agriculture through innovative drip irrigation systems. Everywhere we looked, we saw evidence of human ingenuity adapting to harsh conditions. Communities thrived in places that looked impossible to sustain life, each one a testament to determination and technological innovation.

The contrast between ancient and modern was particularly striking in Jerusalem. In the Old City, we'd see buildings constructed from what they called Jerusalem stone or Israel rock - beautiful beige stone that gave the city its distinctive appearance. These weren't just historic structures; similar materials and techniques were being used in new construction, creating a visual continuity between past and present that few cities manage to achieve.

One trip, when political unrest made our planned excursion to Egypt impossible, we made the bold decision to visit Petra in Jordan instead. This wasn't as simple as changing flights - it meant crossing borders in a region where tensions were high. We had to leave our Israeli bus, walk across a bridge, and find new transportation on the other side. But what awaited us was worth every moment of uncertainty. Petra's buildings, carved directly into rose-colored cliffs, weren't just architectural marvels - they were evidence of an ancient civilization's ingenuity and artistry.

The spiritual dimension of these travels emerged gradually but powerfully. Unlike some who arrived in Israel with firm religious convictions, my faith deepened through experience and observation. I remember my first visit to what was claimed to be Jesus's birthplace - something felt off, didn't give me any real connection. But when I later visited the Church of the Nativity in Bethlehem with NRB, the experience was transformative. You could feel the authenticity of the place, the weight of its history.

Each trip to Israel with the National Religious Broadcasters (NRB) added new layers to my understanding. In the evenings, after days spent exploring sacred sites, we'd gather to watch four broadcasters do their shows live from Israel, sending images and impressions back to American audiences. Being both a participant and witness to how these experiences were shared with others added depth to my own spiritual journey.

The Garden Tomb particularly moved me. While others might debate various holy sites' authenticity, this place carried its own quiet conviction. Walking the same steps where history and faith intersected, seeing the physical evidence of biblical accounts - it made abstract beliefs tangible. These weren't just tourist sites; they were touchstones to something deeper, a growing faith inside me.

Our archaeological work became a form of spiritual practice itself. Working underground in ancient Jewish cities, uncovering rooms where people had lived thousands of years ago, finding artifacts they had touched and used - it created an intimate connection with biblical history. We discovered countless jars, bottles, and everyday items that hadn't seen daylight since biblical times. As Sandy and I worked side by side in these digs, we weren't just uncovering artifacts; we were touching history itself.

The modern Jewish communities we visited showed us how ancient faith adapted to contemporary life. Communes farmed the desert using advanced irrigation systems, proving that spiritual commitment and technological innovation could work hand in hand. Multiple families would live together in these communities, farming the land and maintaining traditions while embracing modern methods. It was a powerful reminder that faith wasn't just about preserving the past - it was about building for the future.

These travels with Duffy's group NRB were more than religious tourism - they were journeys of understanding that changed how I viewed both faith and community. Standing at the Western Wall in Jerusalem, watching people insert their written prayers between the ancient stones, I began to understand faith as something tangible, something that had sustained communities through millennia of challenges. This wasn't the Catholicism of my Denver childhood, with its Latin masses I couldn't understand; this was faith lived out in daily life, in the rhythms of communities both ancient and modern.

The communities we visited in Israel showed me something profound about the connection between faith and activism. Whether it was ancient Jewish settlements we uncovered in archaeological digs or modern kibbutzim making the desert bloom, I saw how belief translated into action. It reminded me of my own work back home - organizing people for causes they believed in, building communities around shared values. The ancient stones we uncovered in our digs might have been different from the political foundations I'd helped build in California, but the principle was the same: people coming together to create something meaningful.

Walking where prophets and disciples had walked, seeing the landscapes that had shaped biblical narratives, brought scripture to life in unexpected ways. But it was the living communities that really captured my attention - the way ancient traditions adapted to modern life without losing their essence. I thought often of my own journey from paper route manager to political organizer to international traveler, how each role had built on what came before while opening new horizons.

Our ventures beyond Israel's borders proved equally enlightening. The journey to Petra came with its own spiritual lessons about trust and courage. Crossing borders in a region of high tension, we had to rely on faith - both spiritual and in each other. The ancient Nabataean civilization that had carved their city from rose-colored cliffs reminded us that human determination, guided by belief, could accomplish seemingly impossible things.

The relationships formed during these travels added another dimension to my faith journey. Sandy and I shared not just hotel rooms and long bus rides, but moments of discovery and wonder. Whether we were digging in archaeological sites or navigating unfamiliar territories, our friendship deepened through shared experience. These bonds of friendship, forged in foreign lands while pursuing spiritual understanding, became another form of faith community.

These journeys beyond America's borders had changed me in ways I couldn't have imagined when I first boarded that plane to Israel. Each trip peeled away another layer of my American-centric viewpoint, revealing a world filled with both struggle and joy, ancient wisdom and modern challenges. The archaeological digs in Israel had taught me that civilization's roots run deep, while my experiences in the modern communes showed me how ancient traditions could adapt to contemporary life without losing their essence.

But perhaps the most profound impact of all this travel was how it shaped my relationships back home. When I returned from these trips, I saw my own community through new eyes. The political work I'd done took on deeper meaning – it wasn't just about local issues anymore, but about our place in an interconnected world. The experiences enriched my relationships with my children and grandchildren, giving me stories to share and perspectives to pass on.

Standing at the Western Wall in Jerusalem or walking among the ancient stones of Petra, I'd often think about the legacy I wanted to leave for my own family. These weren't just tourist destinations; they were touchstones that connected past to present, reminding me that we're all part of a continuing story.

As the century drew to a close, I found myself increasingly drawn to spending time with my growing family. The adventure of international travel had been exhilarating, but now a different kind of journey was calling – watching my grandchildren grow, sharing in their triumphs and challenges, and helping to shape the next generation of our family story.

Life would continue to bless and surprise me with a new chapter called "Grandma".

Chapter 8

FAMILY JOYS AND CHALLENGES

The transition from global traveler to grandmother happened so gradually I barely noticed it at first. One day I was exploring ancient ruins in Israel; the next I was sitting in a Chuck E. Cheese watching Madison, my first great granddaughter, blow out her birthday candles. Life has a way of shifting its focus when you least expect it. But first I had to become a grandmother.

Watching my children become parents themselves was like seeing our family story through a fresh lens. Then watching their children have children was a bigger heart opener.

The transition from mother to grandmother happened on St. Patrick's Day 1983, as Ronald Reagan was gearing up to run for a second term and America was emerging from the recession of the early 80s. Dick Mountjoy was preparing for his next political move to the California State Senate, and our political activities were intensifying. I was at a fundraiser in the Monrovia Hills that evening, discussing campaign strategies and probably not thinking about much beyond the typical pinches and green clothing the holiday brings, when word came that Jennifer had arrived. It was a time of change – not just in my personal life but in California politics as well. Looking back now, it seems fitting that my first grandchild would choose a day when the whole world was already celebrating to make her entrance. The personal and political were always intertwined in my life, and Jennifer's birth marked the beginning of a new chapter for all of us. As Dick's political career was about to soar to new heights in Sacramento, I was embarking on my own new role as grandmother, though I couldn't have known then how profoundly both of these changes would shape the coming decades.

My son, Donnie and my daughter-in-law, Donna, were in Sacramento then, at the beginning of what would become their own journey through military life and frequent moves. It was strange at first, being a grandmother while still relatively young myself. Most of my friends' children were just starting high school, and here I was, holding my first grandchild. But the moment Jennifer was placed in my arms, age became irrelevant. Here was this perfect little being, and I felt that same surge of love I'd experienced with my own children, though somehow different – less wrapped up in responsibility and more purely joyful. Here was this perfect little being, a continuation of our family story, and I felt the same surge of love I'd experienced with my own children.

2 First Borns

Being a grandmother at my age wasn't common, but then nothing about my life had followed the usual script. I'd been a young mother myself, and now here was my son Donnie and his wife Donna, making me a grandmother while I was barely out of young adulthood, but somehow I knew exactly what to do. Each subsequent grandchild brought their own unique joy – Brian with his quiet determination, Stephen with his particular eating habits, and Kim with her spark of independence. They were all so different, yet each one carried something of our family's spirit.

Those early days with Jennifer were different from when I'd been a young mother. As a grandmother, I could savor the moments without the overwhelming responsibility of day-to-day care. Watching Donnie and Donna navigate new parenthood brought back memories of my own learning curve, though their circumstances were quite different. They were in Sacramento then, and I'd make the trip up whenever I could, often on Dick's plane. The military life that had shaped my early motherhood was echoing through to the next generation, as Donnie and Donna would soon be moving with their new baby to Washington D.C.

Two years later, Brian arrived, bringing an entirely different energy to our growing family. From the beginning, he had this quiet determination about him, so different from Jennifer's more reserved nature. I remember my first visit to them in Yugoslavia, little Brian was supposed to sing in the school play. He got up there in front of everyone and simply refused to open his mouth. No amount of coaxing could change his mind. When people went up to ask him why he wouldn't sing, his answer was simple and direct: "Because I don't want to." Even then, he knew his own mind, Gemini as it was!

Those early years with Brian and Jennifer taught me something about being a grandmother that no one had ever told me – how to balance love and discipline from a different angle. I remember a time in Yugoslavia when Brian was acting up at dinner in the hotel restaurant. The men all ate in the dining room, but families weren't typically welcome there. Because we were Americans, they made an exception. When Brian started crying and making a fuss, I took him upstairs to our room. showed him the room key and said we wouldn't go back down until he settled down. That key became our signal throughout the rest of the trip – just holding it up could quiet him. It wasn't about threats; it was about establishing understanding and boundaries.

Grandma Peggy

Jennifer was different. Quiet, introverted, she tried so hard to please everyone. I remember a time when she tried out for cheerleading at Burk High School in Texas. She and her friend Dana both gave it their all, but neither made the squad. The wailing and crying in that gym that day would break anyone's heart, especially a grandmothers. It was one of those moments when being a grandmother meant wanting to fix everything while knowing you couldn't – and shouldn't. These disappointments, as painful as they were to watch, were part of growing up.

Then came Stephen, and with him came an entirely new set of challenges and joys. That birth itself was dramatic – there were complications, and they had to do an emergency C-section. When they got to him, the umbilical cord had become an issue. They had to move quickly, and in the process, he got a cut on his little head. The doctors assured us it wasn't serious, but for Lauri, any mark on her new baby was cause for concern.

Stephen developed his own unique personality early on. The story about his eating habits became family legend – how I supposedly ruined him with one sugar sandwich. The truth is, he was a particularly choosy eater, and one day when he was staying with me, he refused everything I offered. In desperation, I suggested a sugar sandwich, something he'd never had before. His eyes lit up at the novelty, and he actually ate it. From then on, according to family lore, I was responsible for his picky eating habits, though he really only had that one sugar sandwich. He did eventually develop a strong preference for macaroni and cheese, which became his staple.

Stephen Sugar Sandwich

Kim came last, completing the grandchildren circle. By then, the world was settling into the 1980s, with all its changes and complexities. But inside our family, time moved at its own pace, marked by birthdays, holidays, and those special moments that bind generations together.

The grandchildren's visits to my house in Monrovia were always eventful. I remember when Stephen would come over, and even though he was particular about his food, he brought such joy with his presence. The macaroni and cheese phase lasted until he was sixteen, but it never affected his growth – he grew tall and strong despite his limited menu.

Then came the next generation. I had never imagined being a great grandmother and it was a bit of a surprise to all of us. But the best surprise ever! My first great granddaughter Madison arrived on September 10, 2001, just one day before the world would change forever. Jennifer was in the hospital during the World Trade Tower devastation, frustrated that there was nothing else on television besides coverage of the collapse. While the world outside was in chaos, inside that hospital room, we were celebrating new life. It was a few years before I would see the next great granddaughter but she came in with another special date to remind us all of her presence.

Jennifer's next daughter, Riley, sticking with tradition being born on a holiday or world changing event. Her Christmas Eve arrival, 2010 brought the whole family together in a small house, in Denver where Jennifer and Marshall (Jennifer's husband) had been getting ready for their growing family. With blow-up beds covering every inch of floor space, our entire family converged. The timing seemed perfect – a holiday baby when everyone could be there to celebrate. Jennifer came home to a house full of people, which might not have been ideal for a new mother, but it was how our family operated – always together, always celebrating.

The next great granddaughter, Ella, born 6/18/12 and then Cecilia born in quick succession on 2/16/15 rounded out Jennifer's growing family. Jennifer had barely finished with Ella when Cecilia was on the way. I remember her nursing them both at the same time, proving that mothers can do whatever they need to do. The girls have grown into their own distinct personalities – Ella with her theatrical talents, Riley the artist and Cecilia with her own special spark. Jennifer would prove to be a natural mother as she grew, her children – Madison, Riley, Ella, and Cecilia – each arriving with their own personalities fully formed, keeping us all on our toes.

Watching these great-grandchildren grow has been different from my earlier experiences as a grandmother. The world they're growing up in barely resembles the one I knew. They have their tablets and phones, technologies we couldn't have imagined back when we were organizing PTA carnivals and making phone calls from landlines. Sometimes when they visit, they're all on their devices, and I miss the simple interactions we used to have. But then I see them in theater productions, or watch them performing, and I realize they're finding their own ways to connect and create.

Looking at all of them now – my children, grandchildren, and great-grandchildren – I see pieces of our family history in each of their faces. Jennifer has become such a devoted mother, guiding her own children through their challenges and triumphs. Brian and Stephen have grown into men and husbands any grandmother would be proud of, and Kim has found her special soul mate.

The world keeps changing around us. These children will never know what it was like to grow up without computers or cell phones. They won't experience the simple joy of a paper route or understand why making your own clothes was such a necessity. But they're creating their own memories, their own traditions.

I've learned that being a grandmother, and now a great-grandmother, isn't about holding onto the past. It's about bridging it to the future, sharing what wisdom we can while accepting that each generation must find its own way. I know that our family story continues to unfold in ways I never could have imagined.

The love flows both ways. The grandchildren and great-grandchildren keep me young in their own way, even as I slow down. They help me navigate this new digital world, though I still prefer my simpler ways. And while I might not always understand their music or their technology, I understand their hearts. That's what matters most.

As I watch this fourth generation growing up, I'm filled with hope and curiosity about where their paths will lead. Will they inherit our family's tendency to forge our own ways? Will they carry forward the values and traditions we've tried to instill? Only time will tell, but I know they'll make their own unique marks on the world, just as each generation before them has done.

What amazes me most is watching how traits and tendencies echo through the generations. Jennifer's children have inherited that creative spark, though it shows itself differently in each of them. The theater, singing and art has become their outlet – something I wish we'd had access to in my day.

I've been so blessed to have attended weddings of my children, grandchildren and who knows perhaps a great granddaughter.

When Stephen married his beautiful bride, Martyna, in Newport Beach California on Valentines Day 2020, our family was melded with a Polish family in a genuine melting of two cultures. Little did we know that the world was about to change again. By the time we returned to our small town in Texas, the entire world had shut down.

Life went on as usual thankfully, even though I was in one of the most susceptible demographics to contract Covid. My family in Texas weathered the world crisis the same way we have always done, TOGETHER!

The whole family held our breath as we wondered if Brian who had grown into such a fiercely independent, yet caring man would ever settle down and get married. He has grown into such a caring man and when I noticed how he opened car doors for me, something he must have learned from watching his father do the same thing, I would beam with pride. These small gestures of respect and care show me that despite all the changes in the world, some important values have carried through to the next generation. He is truly a Dobbins. When he brought Jenn to meet the family I can only imagine her overwhelm with our brood.

The moment came that Jenn and Brian, delivered the news of their soon to be born daughter Charlotte. In traditional Dobbins fashion the order may not have been traditional, but love was the thread that bound them together. I became a great grandmother again on November 16, 2023 another holiday gift this time Thanksgiving. I could not have had more to be grateful for and then Charlotte.

The relationship between my grandchildren has evolved over time. Jennifer started out so reserved, while Brian was more outgoing, involved in bowling and baseball, always with his group of friends. Now I watch the great-grandchildren developing their own personalities and interests.

My role has shifted too. When the kids come over now, it's different from those early days of babysitting and sugar sandwiches. Sometimes it can be overwhelming when they're all here, playing games on their phones, the noise level rising. But I've learned to cherish these moments, even if I sometimes need to head home early when it gets to be too much.

Family gatherings have changed over the years. I remember when we could all fit around one table, and now we need multiple rooms just to contain everyone. But that's the beauty of family – it grows and changes, each new addition bringing their own flavor to our story.

Looking at all of them now – my children, grandchildren, and great-grandchildren – I see pieces of our family history in each of their faces

The great-grandchildren are growing up in a world I barely recognize, yet they still carry pieces of our family's past. These little echoes of resemblance remind me how family ties endure, even as each generation forges its own path.

Those early days weren't easy for Jennifer reminding me of my own youth of being a mom – having Madison while still so young herself, then Riley, Ella, and Cecilia coming in quick succession. But she's found her own way of parenting, different from how we did things but effective for today's world. She manages their activities, their performances, their schedules with a grace I admire.

The contrast between my early grand mothering days and now is striking. When Jennifer and Brian were little, visiting them meant traveling to Yugoslavia or Canada, navigating international moves and military life. Now, having family close by is a blessing, even if our time together looks different than it used to. The great-grandchildren pop in and out, always in motion, always connected to their devices, but still bringing that special energy that only young people can bring.

Sometimes I think about how different their childhood is from mine, or even from their parents' generation. They'll never know what it's like to wait for a weekly market day to get fresh food, like I experienced in Yugoslavia. They won't understand the excitement of a family camping trip in a station wagon, or the adventure of making your own clothes because store-bought ones were too expensive. Their world is full of immediate gratification and constant connectivity.

Yet despite all these changes, the core of what makes our family special remains the same. The love, the support, the way we come together in times of celebration and challenge – these things transcend generations. When I watch Madison with her sisters, I see the same protective instinct I felt toward my own brother. When I hear them laugh together, it reminds me of the joy that family can bring, no matter what era we're living in.

The years have taught me that being a grandmother, and now a great-grandmother, isn't about trying to recreate the past or impose our old ways on the new generation. It's about adapting, understanding, and finding ways to connect across differences. Sometimes that means learning to text or trying to understand their online worlds. Other times it means simply being present, offering the kind of unconditional love that never goes out of style.

Each generation faces its own challenges. I watch these children navigating a world that seems to change faster every day, and I marvel at their adaptability. They're growing up in an era where technology dominates everything, where the simple pleasures we once knew have been replaced by digital alternatives. Yet they still find ways to create, to perform, to connect with each other and with us.

As I look at our expanding family tree, I'm filled with pride and wonder. From those first days with Jennifer as my only grandchild to now, when the great-grandchildren fill the house with their energy and noise, each addition has brought new joy, new challenges, and new opportunities to love. The family story continues to unfold, each generation writing its own chapter while building on the foundation we laid so many years ago.

Life has a way of coming full circle in the most unexpected ways. Looking back now, I can hardly believe how far we've come from those early days when I was just a teenage mother myself, with only my own mom, Grammie and Bapa for family support. I remember the uncertainty of those times – young, married to Jerry, navigating military life with a growing family. But somehow, through all the moves and challenges, we created something beautiful.

Now I sit here, seeing my grandchildren become parents themselves, watching my great-grandchildren perform in their plays, and I'm struck by how this family has blossomed. From those humble beginnings in military housing, counting every penny of the monthly allowance, to now having this expansive, vibrant family that fills entire rooms during holidays – it's more than I could have dreamed possible.

The transformation amazes me. My own early experiences of motherhood were about survival and determination, making do with what we had. Now I watch Jennifer juggling activities and performances, managing a household full of creative, energetic daughters. I see Brian and Stephen, married and Stephen living abroad, showing such care and consideration, qualities that would have made their grandfather proud. Even when I feel overwhelmed by their technology and fast-paced lives, I can't help but marvel at how each generation builds upon what came before, creating their own unique way of being family.

Yet despite all these changes, the core of what makes our family special remains the same. The love, the support, the way we come together in times of celebration and challenge – these things transcend generations. When I hear them laugh together, it reminds me of the joy that family can bring, no matter what era we're living in.

The years have taught me that being a grandmother, and now a great-grandmother, isn't about trying to recreate the past or impose our old ways on the new generation. It's about adapting, understanding, and finding ways to connect across the differences.

Sometimes, sitting in my chair while they all buzz around me with their phones and tablets, I think about that young girl I once was, standing in front of a house in my lime green shirt, not knowing that a passing car would lead to all of this. From four children of my own to grandchildren to great-grandchildren – each one adding their own thread to our family tapestry. It's not the way I imagined it back then, but it's turned out more beautiful than any plan I could have made.

They may not understand what it means to load up a station wagon for camping or to make your own clothes, but they understand love and family in their own way. And maybe that's the greatest gift of all – seeing how love grows and changes but never diminishes, passing from one generation to the next, each time creating something new and wonderful.

As I watch these great-grandchildren pursuing their theatrical passions, I see echoes of the creativity that has always run through our family. Though their outlets may be different from the ways I expressed myself – through sewing, crafting, and organizing events – that same spark burns bright. In many ways, my journey from young mother making clothes with one bolt of fabric, to political organizer planning major events prepared me for this final act, though I never could have predicted where life would lead.

4 Generations

Chapter 9

A LIFE'S THREAD

The first time I made a dress, I didn't even have a sewing machine. It was just me, a pattern, and determination – the same determination that would later help me organize political campaigns and eventually lead me to become known as "the button lady" in a whole new community. Looking back now, I can see how each creative pursuit and organizational challenge was preparing me for what would come next.

Those early days of sewing out of necessity taught me more than just how to follow a pattern. When you're making clothes for four children, you learn to be resourceful, to see possibilities where others might see limitations. I'd buy bolts of fabric and make matching outfits – Donnie and Jerry would get a shirt, and the girls would get their dresses. It wasn't just about saving money; it was about creating something personal, something that bound us together as a family.

This same creative spirit would later express itself in different ways – through flower arranging classes, through organizing Republican events, through making buttons for candidates I believed in. Each pursuit added another dimension to who I was becoming, though I didn't realize it at the time. The skills I learned making bows and arranging flowers would come in handy years later when I was creating gift baskets for political fundraisers and arranging the flowers for my daughters' weddings.

Spring 2016 brought seismic changes to both the political landscape and my personal journey. As Donald Trump was securing the Republican nomination, shaking up the establishment and speaking to the issues I'd championed for decades, I made the boldest decision of my life - leaving my California home of

55 years to start fresh in Texas. The irony wasn't lost on me; at nearly 80 years old, when most people are settling into familiar routines, I was packing up for a cross-country move once again. This move was different than the young girl from Denver in a bus with her mother to California. This was my choice and excitement surrounded every moment of it.

Some may have thought I was crazy, of course. Leaving my home in Monrovia, where I'd lived independently for 37 years, to move to a small town in Texas seemed risky at my age. But I'd never been one to let age dictate my choices. The promise of living near family in Wichita Falls and the pull of a new adventure proved stronger than any doubts.

True to form, I didn't waste any time getting involved in local politics. While others might have taken months to settle in, I found the Republican headquarters within my first week. They needed help with the Trump campaign, and I knew exactly what I could contribute. I'd brought my button-making equipment from California, and before long, my dining room became a production center for campaign buttons. The designs were simple at first - just Trump's name and basic slogans. But as demand grew, so did my creativity.

Word spread quickly in our small community. People started coming by specifically requesting "the Button Lady's" latest designs. What had started as a way to stay involved became my new identity. In California, I'd been known for organizing events and running campaigns. Here in Texas, I was becoming known for creating tangible symbols of political support that people wore proudly. Every button that went out carried a piece of my passion for the causes I believed in.

Starting over at 80 might seem daunting to most, but this transition felt natural. Wichita Falls, with its slower pace and traditional values, reminded me of the America I'd always fought to preserve. Setting up a Republican headquarters modeled on everything I'd learned in California gave me purpose, while making buttons kept my creative spirit alive.

The irony wasn't lost on me when my eyesight began failing while helping Debbie prepare Memorial Day flags to plant in 1,000 homes in our neighborhood. Here I was, doing what I'd always done – throwing myself into a community project, being creative, organizing and contributing – when life decided to throw me its latest curve ball. A thousand flags needed planting around the neighborhood, and suddenly my eye sight was gone. A sroke in my retina stopped me in my tracks. It was almost a year later before some of my sight returned.

This was after I'd established myself in Texas, after I'd set up a Republican headquarters modeled on everything I'd learned in California, after I'd become known as the button lady who could create whatever design was needed for Trump supporters. I'd come to Texas at 80 years old with the same independent spirit that had driven me all my life – from that teenage girl making her first dress without a sewing machine to the grandmother organizing political rallies and making campaign buttons.

The transition wasn't easy. When you've spent your whole life being the one others depend on, accepting help doesn't come naturally. Driving had been my freedom, my way of staying connected and involved. Each time I got in the car to go to headquarters or to make a supply run for more button materials, I was maintaining my independence. But gradually, the signs became impossible to ignore. Street signs blurred, and the confidence I'd always felt behind the wheel began to waver.

People had always said I was creative in finding solutions, but this challenge required a different kind of creativity. How do you stay relevant when you can't see to make the buttons that had become your trademark? How do you maintain your independence when you can't drive to the activities that filled your days? These weren't questions I'd ever expected to face, yet here they were, demanding answers.

The hardest part wasn't the physical recovery – though that was challenging enough. It was accepting that my fiercely guarded independence was slipping away, one small surrender at a time. After months of doctor visits, my vision slowly improved, though not enough to completely ease my family's concerns about my driving. But you don't spend decades being the family matriarch, the organizer, the doer, just to suddenly become passive. So yes, I probably drove when I shouldn't have, holding onto that last thread of independence like a lifeline.

My vanity and stubbornness showed in small ways – refusing to use a cane, preferring instead to lean on a shopping cart when I went to the store. I'd always been the one helping others; accepting help myself felt like admitting defeat. But life wasn't finished teaching me its lessons. Just as my eyesight was improving, the first fall changed everything. Breaking my ankle might seem like a simple injury, but at my age, it meant months of rehabilitation.

Living next door to family turned out to be a blessing I hadn't fully appreciated until then. During those months of recovery, they moved in to care for me, and I had to face a truth I'd been avoiding: life was changing, whether I was ready or not. The walker I'd avoided "like the plague" became my constant companion. Each step with it felt like a reminder of my new reality.

For someone who had spent her life making things happen – from sewing dresses without a machine to organizing political campaigns, from raising four children to becoming the button lady of Texas – this new dependency was harder to accept than any physical limitation. The woman who had once walked precincts and organized rallies now had to ask for help getting to the bathroom. Yet in this challenge, I discovered something unexpected: my family's strength reflected back the same resilience I'd always tried to instill in them.

That moment of resistance, lying on my bedroom floor after following minor falls, refusing to call for help – it perfectly captured the struggle between who I'd always been and who I was becoming. My family's growing frustration with my stubbornness was rooted in love, I knew that, but old habits and old pride die hard. I didn't want to disrupt their lives, didn't want those midnight calls for help to become their new normal.

Then came the ice cream incident. Such a simple thing, fixing myself a bowl of ice cream, turning too quickly back to the fridge, (something I'd done thousands of times before) and in an instant I found myself crumpled on the floor of my kitchen. But this fall was different. The impact of hitting the floor, my shoulder and pelvis taking the brunt of it, marked a turning point I couldn't ignore. It wasn't just another fall I could brush off and keep to myself.

The emergency room brought the starkest reality check yet. As doctors attempted to relocate my dislocated shoulder, my body had other plans. I wasn't aware when my CO_2 levels plummeted, wasn't conscious to see my son's face as he watched the color drain from mine. He had to witness what I couldn't – the moment when my mortality became undeniably real, would he be watching his mother pass away? The fractured pelvis and shoulder that wouldn't relocate weren't just injuries to recover from; they were messengers delivering a truth I'd been trying to outrun: my independence, at least as I'd known it, was nearly over.

This new chapter wasn't optional, and it wasn't temporary. It demanded not just physical healing but a complete reimagining of how I would live. The woman who had once organized political campaigns, made thousands of buttons, organized fundraisers and Bingo games, flew in private planes around California and fiercely guarded her independence now had to learn a different kind of strength – the strength to accept help, to let my family step into the caregiver role, to find new ways to matter that didn't depend on doing everything myself.

The conflicts among my children over my care weren't surprising – they're all strong-willed, just like their mother. Each had their own vision of what was best for me, drawn from their own experiences and concerns. But just as I'd done throughout my life, I maintained my right to chart my own course, even if that course now involved a lift chair and walker.

It was during one of those low moments, sitting with Debbie, that I uttered words I never thought I'd say: "I'm not good for anything." Her reaction – immediate and fierce – shook me out of my self-pity. She helped me see that "doing" wasn't the only way to matter. Being the matriarch, maintaining my political passion even from my lift chair, sharing wisdom with my grandchildren and great-grandchildren – these were valuable contributions too.

My friends from across the country still call, eager to discuss the latest political developments. What a joy to witness Trump's presidency unfold, validating decades of grassroots activism. Even if I can't make buttons anymore, I can still engage in the political discourse that has been such a vital part of my life.

This transition into accepting care while maintaining my essential self has taught me perhaps the most important lesson of my life: our worth isn't measured by what we do, but by who we are and how we influence those around us. As I watch my family navigate these changes with me, I see the strength and resilience I tried to instill in them reflected back. Perhaps this is what a life well lived really means – not just the doing, but the being, the loving, and the leaving of a legacy that continues through generations.

Peggy, The Matriarch

Chapter 10

LESSONS FROM NINE DECADES

November 4, 2024, Donald Trump was elected as the 47th President of the United States. Sitting in my lift chair, watching the results come in, I felt a profound sense of validation. For eight years, I'd been championing him, making buttons, organizing support – even when my eyesight began to fail and my mobility became limited. This victory represented everything I'd worked for throughout my political life, from those early days walking precincts to organizing rallies and events.

The timing seems perfect for reflection. At 87, I've learned that life's greatest lessons often come when you least expect them, and sometimes in packages you'd rather not open. These past few years have taught me more about grace and acceptance than all my previous decades combined. While I may not be able to make campaign buttons anymore or drive myself to political meetings, my passion for what I believe in hasn't dimmed one bit.

My greatest lesson has been understanding that influence doesn't always require action. Sometimes it's about being present, being steady, being an example of resilience in the face of change. I've watched my family rally around me, each in their own way, and seen how the strength I tried to instill in them has come full circle. They're not just caring for me; they're carrying forward the values and determination that have always defined our family.

The political activism that has been such a crucial part of my life continues, just in a different form. Instead of organizing events, I'm sharing wisdom. Instead of walking precincts, I'm making phone calls. My lift chair has become my command center, and from here, I can still participate in the causes I believe in, still contribute to the conversations that matter.

From that young girl in Denver sneaking into movie theaters, to the paper lady supporting her family, to the political organizer who would help shape California politics, to the button lady of Texas – each chapter of my life has built upon the last. Through every transition, every challenge, every triumph, certain truths have remained constant: the importance of family, the power of determination, and the need to stand up for what you believe in.

Now, watching Trump's victory from my lift chair, I see how all the pieces fit together. Those early lessons in resourcefulness – sewing without a machine, making do with what we had – prepared me for a lifetime of finding creative solutions. The independence I developed as a young mother translated into political activism, and that same spirit now helps me navigate the challenges of aging.

My family has grown beyond anything I could have imagined during those early days in military housing. Four children became grandchildren, then great-grandchildren, each generation adding their own colors to our family tapestry. Watching them pursue their dreams – whether on stage, in politics, or in their personal lives – I see echoes of the determination that has always run through our family line.

Yes, life looks different now. The walker I once resisted has become a constant companion, and my lift chair serves as my new headquarters. But from here, I still wage my campaigns – for family, for politics, for what's right. The methods may have changed, but the mission remains the same.

If there's one thing I've learned in my 87 years, it's that life isn't about maintaining control – it's about adapting to change while holding onto your core values. My worth isn't measured by my mobility or independence, but by the love I've given, the family I've nurtured, and the causes I've championed.

Looking back, I see that every challenge was preparing me for what came next. Each role I played – daughter, wife, mother, grandmother, great-grandmother, political activist, community organizer – added another layer to who I would become. Even these recent years, learning to accept help instead of always being the helper, have taught me valuable lessons about grace and humility.

The victory of our 47th President, Donald Trump I just witnessed from my lift chair, represents more than just political triumph. It represents the power of persistence, the importance of standing firm in your beliefs, and the way life can surprise you with joy even in its later chapters. While I may not be making campaign buttons anymore, my influence continues through the values I've passed down, the wisdom I share, and the example I set of never giving up on what matters most.

They say life comes full circle, and perhaps that's true. That teenage girl who once sewed dresses without a machine would hardly recognize the great-grandmother watching her great-grandchildren. But she would recognize the spirit – that unchanging core of determination, love, and purpose that has carried me through nine decades of living, learning, and growing.

As I sit here in my lift chair, surrounded by family, still engaged in the political discourse I love, still offering guidance and wisdom to those who seek it, I realize that this isn't an ending – it's just another beginning. The story continues through my children, grandchildren, and great-grandchildren, each carrying forward pieces of the legacy we've built together.

Life well lived isn't about the positions we hold or the things we accomplish – though I'm proud of those. It's about the lives we touch, the values we uphold, and the love we share. By that measure, I can look back on these nine decades with satisfaction, knowing that while my journey has had its share of challenges, it has been rich with purpose, love, and meaning.

As I watch this new chapter of American history unfold, I'm grateful for my front-row seat to witness it. More than that, I'm grateful for the journey that brought me here – every step, every struggle, every joy. This is what a life well lived looks like: not perfect, not always easy, but always true to itself, always reaching for something better, always connected to what matters most.

The story isn't over yet. There are still political discussions to have, family moments to cherish, and wisdom to share. And while I may need help getting around these days, my spirit remains as independent and determined as ever. That, perhaps, is my greatest legacy – showing that no matter what life throws at you, you can adapt and grow while staying true to who you are.

Chapter 11

FINAL CHAPTER
AN INCREDIBLE LIFE'S JOURNEY

As I sit here, looking back on my 87 years, I can't help but marvel at the journey life has taken me on. From a young girl in Denver to a political activist in California, and now settling into my golden years in Texas, it's been quite the ride. I've seen the world change in ways I never could have imagined, and I've changed right along with it. But through it all, there's been one constant - my love for life and the people in it.

You know, when you're young, you think you've got it all figured out. I remember being a teenager, thinking I knew everything there was to know about the world. Boy, was I wrong! But that's the beauty of life, isn't it? You never stop learning, never stop growing. And let me tell you, I've done plenty of both.

I've always been a bit of a go-getter, never one to sit still for too long. Even as a young girl, I was always looking for the next adventure. I remember when I first moved to California with my mom. It was a whole new world, and I was ready to take it on. I didn't have much, but I had determination, and that's worth more than gold in my book.

Looking back, I realize now that those early years really shaped who I became. Moving around, having to adapt to new situations - it taught me to be flexible, to roll with the punches. And let me tell you, life's thrown plenty of punches my way. But you know what? I'm still standing, and I'm proud of that.

One of the biggest lessons I've learned is the importance of family. Now, don't get me wrong, we've had our ups and downs. What family doesn't? But at the end of the day, family is what matters most. I look at my children, my grandchildren, even my great-grandchildren, and I see the legacy I'm leaving behind. It's not about money or possessions. It's about the love we share, the memories we've made, and the values we pass on.

I remember when I first became a grandmother. Oh, what a day that was! I held little Jennifer in my arms, and it was like falling in love all over again. Being a grandmother is a special kind of joy. You get all the fun of parenting without the sleepless nights and dirty diapers! Well, most of the time, anyway.

You know, people often ask me about my involvement in politics. They want to know what drove me to get so involved. The truth is, it wasn't something I planned. It just sort of happened. But once I got started, there was no stopping me. I believed - still believe - in the power of ordinary people to make a difference. That's what kept me going all those years, knocking on doors, making phone calls, organizing events. It wasn't always easy, but it was always worth it.

I remember one time, we were working on a campaign - I can't even remember which one now, there were so many - and things weren't looking good. We were behind in the polls, low on funds, and morale was dropping. But you know what? We didn't give up. We worked harder, stayed later, pushed ourselves to the limit. And in the end, we won. That taught me a valuable lesson: never underestimate the power of determination and hard work.

Of course, life hasn't always been about politics and campaigns. I've had my fair share of personal struggles too. There were times when money was tight, when relationships were strained, when health issues seemed overwhelming. But you know what? I got through it all. And I didn't do it alone. I had my faith, my family, and my friends to lean on. That's another lesson I've learned: it's okay to ask for help. We're not meant to go through life alone.

One of the greatest joys in my life has been travel. Oh, the places I've been! Israel, Greece, Ireland, Yugoslavia, Canada, Hawaii - each place left its mark on me. I remember standing at the Western Wall in Jerusalem, feeling the weight of history all around me. Or walking through the streets of Athens, imagining the ancient philosophers who once walked those same paths. Travel broadens your horizons, opens your mind to new ideas and perspectives. It's something I wish everyone could experience.

You know, as you get older, you start to see things differently. The little things that used to bother you don't seem so important anymore. Instead, you learn to appreciate the small joys in life. A cup of coffee in the morning, a phone call from a grandchild, a beautiful sunset - these are the things that matter.

I've also learned the importance of staying active, both physically and mentally. Even now, I try to keep busy. Whether it's making phone calls to friends, donating to political causes or just keeping up with the news, I believe it's important to stay engaged with the world around you. It keeps you young, keeps you sharp.

Of course, aging isn't always easy. There are days when my body doesn't want to cooperate, when my eyesight isn't what it used to be. But you know what? I'm grateful for every day I have. Each morning I wake up is a gift, and I try to make the most of it.

One thing I've noticed as I've gotten older is how much the world has changed. Technology, in particular, has transformed everything. I remember when having a television was a big deal. Now, everyone's walking around with computers in their pockets! It can be a bit overwhelming at times, but I try to keep up. After all, you're never too old to learn something new.

Speaking of learning, that's another piece of advice I'd give to anyone: never stop learning. Whether it's picking up a new hobby, reading a book on a subject you know nothing about, or just talking to people with different experiences - there's always something new to discover. Life is a continuous education, and the world is our classroom.

Looking back on my life, I'm amazed at all I've accomplished. Not because I think I'm special, but because I never let fear hold me back. Whether it was moving to a new city, taking on a challenging job, or standing up for what I believed in, I always tried to face my fears head-on. And you know what? More often than not, things worked out just fine.

That's not to say I haven't made mistakes. Oh boy, have I made some doozies! But that's part of life too. The important thing is to learn from your mistakes, to use them as stepping stones rather than stumbling blocks. I've tried to teach my children and grandchildren that it's okay to fail sometimes. What matters is that you pick yourself up and try again.

You know, as I sit here thinking about my life, I realize how blessed I've been. Not because everything's been perfect - far from it! But because I've had the opportunity to live a full life, to love and be loved, to make a difference in my own small way. And really, what more can anyone ask for?

If I could give any advice to the younger generations, it would be this: live with purpose. Find something you're passionate about and pursue it with all your heart. For me, it was politics and community service. For you, it might be something entirely different. But whatever it is, throw yourself into it. Life is too short for half-measures.

I'd also say this: cherish your relationships. In the end, it's not the money you've made or the things you've accumulated that matter. It's the people you've loved, the lives you've touched. I look at my family - my children, grandchildren, great-grandchildren - and I see my greatest legacy. If I've done nothing else in this life, I've loved them fiercely and unconditionally. And that, to me, is success.

Another piece of advice: stay curious. The world is full of wonders, big and small. Never lose your sense of awe, your desire to learn and explore. Whether it's trying a new recipe, visiting a new place, or learning about a different culture - keep pushing your boundaries. Life is an adventure, and it's up to us to make the most of it.

I've also learned the importance of forgiveness. Lord knows I've had my share of disagreements and falling outs over the years. But holding onto anger and resentment only hurts yourself in the long run. Learning to forgive - not just others, but also yourself - is one of the most freeing things you can do.

You know, people often talk about leaving a legacy. For a long time, I thought that meant doing something big and grand, something that would put your name in the history books. But as I've gotten older, I've realized that legacy is about the small things too. It's about the values you instill in your children, the kindness you show to strangers, the little ways you make the world a better place each day.

I look at the world today, and sometimes it can seem pretty scary. There's so much division, so much anger. But you know what? I still have hope. Because I've seen the goodness in people, the incredible things we can accomplish when we work together. I've seen it in my community, in my country, and in my travels around the world. And that gives me hope for the future.

As I near the end of my journey, I find myself reflecting more and more on the life I've lived. And you know what? I wouldn't change a thing. Oh sure, there are things I might have done differently if I had known then what I know now. But every experience, every triumph and every setback, has shaped me into the person I am today. And I'm pretty darn proud of that person.

I've lived through wars and economic depressions, through cultural revolutions and technological transformations. I've seen man walk on the moon and computers shrink from room-sized machines to devices that fit in your pocket. Through it all, I've tried to keep an open mind, to embrace change rather than fear it. It hasn't always been easy, but it's made life a whole lot more interesting.

You know, they say wisdom comes with age. I don't know if I'd call myself wise, but I've certainly learned a thing or two over the years. I've learned that kindness matters more than being right. That a good laugh can cure a multitude of ills. That the best way to find yourself is to lose yourself in service to others.

I've learned that life is precious and fleeting. That each day is a gift, not a guarantee. I've learned to appreciate the simple things - a warm cup of coffee in the morning, a phone call from a loved one, the feel of the sun on my face. These are the things that make life rich and beautiful.

As I look to the future, I'm filled with a sense of anticipation. Not for myself - my big adventures are behind me now. But for my children, grandchildren, and great-grandchildren. I'm excited to see what they'll accomplish, how they'll shape the world. I hope they'll remember the stories I've told them, the lessons I've tried to impart. But more than that, I hope they'll forge their own paths, create their own stories.

You know, people often talk about the "good old days," as if everything was better in the past. But I don't believe that. Sure, some things were simpler back then. But the world has made incredible progress too. We've made strides in civil rights, in medicine, in technology. We've opened up opportunities that were once unimaginable. The world my great-grandchildren are growing up in is full of possibilities. And that fills me with joy.

Of course, there are challenges too. The world faces problems that my generation couldn't have imagined. Global pandemics, divisive ness in our country and the rapid pace of technological change - these are big, complex issues. But I have faith in the younger generations. They're smart, they're passionate, and they care deeply about making the world a better place. I believe they're up to the challenge.

As for me, well, I'm content. I've lived a full life, a life of purpose and meaning. I've loved and been loved. I've made my mark, in my own small way. And now, I'm ready for whatever comes next. I face the future with curiosity and peace, grateful for the life I've lived and the people I've shared it with.

You know, they say life is a journey, not a destination. And what a journey it's been! From that little girl in Denver to the woman I am today, it's been quite the ride. There have been ups and downs, twists and turns I never saw coming. But through it all, I've tried to keep moving forward, to keep growing and learning.

As I wrap up these reflections, I want to leave you with this thought: Life is a precious gift. It's messy and complicated and sometimes downright difficult. But it's also beautiful and surprising and filled with wonder. So live it fully. Love deeply. Take risks. Stand up for what you believe in. Be kind. And above all, never stop growing, never stop learning, never stop embracing the adventure that is life.

To my family, my friends, and all those who have been part of my journey - thank you. You've enriched my life in ways I can't even begin to express. And to those who come after me - my grandchildren, great-grandchildren, and beyond - remember this: You carry within you the hopes and dreams of all those who came before. Honor that legacy, but don't be bound by it. Write your own story. Make it a good one.

And so, as I close this chapter of reflections, I do so with a heart full of gratitude, a mind full of memories, and a spirit still eager for whatever adventures tomorrow may bring. Life has been good to me, and I am thankful for every moment of it. Here's to the journey - past, present, and future. May it always be filled with love, laughter, and the joy of discovery.

ABOUT THE AUTHOR

Debbie Dobbins is a natural-born storyteller with a gift for capturing the essence of the human spirit. As the daughter of Peggy Mew, she had a front-row seat to one of the most remarkable life stories of resilience and determination she would ever encounter. Growing up in a household where politics, community service, and fierce independence were daily lessons, Debbie absorbed not just the events but the energy and spirit that made her mother's life so extraordinary.

This biography emerged from months of intimate conversations between mother and daughter in 2024. Drawing on her experience as an author and transformational teacher, Debbie approached this project not just as a chronicler of events, but as a daughter seeking to preserve the wisdom, humor, and indomitable spirit of a woman who helped shape California politics while raising four children and forging her own path.

What began as a simple desire to record her mother's memories evolved into a profound journey of discovery. Through their conversations, Debbie uncovered layers of her mother's story that even she, having lived through much of it, had never fully appreciated. Her ability to weave together historical events, personal anecdotes, and family dynamics brings her mother's story to life with authenticity and heart.

Currently dividing her time between Texas and the Caribbean, Debbie has published several books on personal transformation and prosperity consciousness. However, this biography stands apart as a labor of love - a daughter's tribute to her mother's extraordinary journey from a spirited young girl in Denver to a matriarch overseeing four generations in Texas.

When not writing or teaching, Debbie can be found enjoying morning coffee rituals, often reflecting on the lessons learned from her mother about independence, resilience, and the power of staying true to oneself. This biography represents not just a daughter's gift to her mother, but a gift to future generations who will find inspiration in Peggy Mew's remarkable story.

FAMILY TREE OF MATRIARCH

Peggy Mew

Born 2/3/37

Second Generation:

Deborah Suzanne Dobbins—6/3/55

Cynthia Lynn Dobbins—5/17/57

Donald Glen Dobbins—12/15/58

Laura Gay Dobbins—2/26/61

Third Generation:

Jennifer Dobbins—3/17/83

Brian Dobbins—6/10/1985

Stephen McCormick—8/22/94

Kimberly McCormick—6/30/94

Four Generation:

Madison Dobbins—9/10/01

Riley Collins—12/24/2010

Ella Collins—6/18/12

Cecilia Collins—2/16/15

Charlotte Dobbins—11/16/23

PICTURES

Made in the USA
Columbia, SC
11 February 2025

53663937R00065